MAR 1 7 2008

P9-DNV-745

WEST LEBANON LIBRARY
57 MAIN STREET
WEST LEBANON, NH 03784

South Korea

South Korea

BY PATRICIA K. KUMMER

Enchantment of the World™
Second Series

Children's Press®

An Imprint of Scholastic Inc.

NEW YORK   TORONTO   LONDON   AUCKLAND   SYDNEY
MEXICO CITY   NEW DELHI   HONG KONG
DANBURY, CONNECTICUT

WEST LEBANON LIBRARY
57 MAIN STREET
WEST LEBANON, NH 03784

Frontispiece: Gyeongbokgung Palace, Seoul

Consultant: Roald Maliangkay, Australian National University Centre for Korean Studies, Canberra, Australia

Please note: All statistics are as up-to-date as possible at the time of publication.

Book production by Herman Adler

Library of Congress Cataloging-in-Publication Data

Kummer, Patricia K.
 South Korea / by Patricia K. Kummer.
    p. cm.—(Enchantment of the world. Second series)
 Includes bibliographical references and index.
 ISBN-13: 978-0-531-18486-8
 ISBN-10: 0-531-18486-2
 1. Korea (South)—Juvenile literature. I. Title.
 DS907.4.K86 2008
 951.95—dc22   2007021403

No part of this publication may be reproduced in whole or in part, or stored in a retrieval system, or transmitted in any form or by any means, electronic, mechanical, photocopying, recording, or otherwise, without written permission of the publisher. For information regarding permission, write to Scholastic Inc., 557 Broadway, New York, NY 10012.

© 2008 by Patricia K. Kummer.
All rights reserved. Published in 2008 by Children's Press, an imprint of Scholastic Inc.
Published simultaneously in Canada.
Printed in the United States of America.   4 4

SCHOLASTIC, CHILDREN'S PRESS, and associated logos are trademarks and/or registered trademarks of Scholastic Inc.
1 2 3 4 5 6 7 8 9 10 R 17 16 15 14 13 12 11 10 09 08   08

Acknowledgments

I would like to thank the Chicago staffs of the (South) Korean Consulate and the (South) Korean National Tourism Organization for their generous help. In addition, I extend my special thanks to the staff of the Lisle Library District for giving me access to the library's Asian art collection and to my son Kristopher Kummer for photographing me with these items for the photo at the end of this book.

Contents

Cover photo:
South Korean
ceremonial guard

Traditional dancers

Ceramic jar

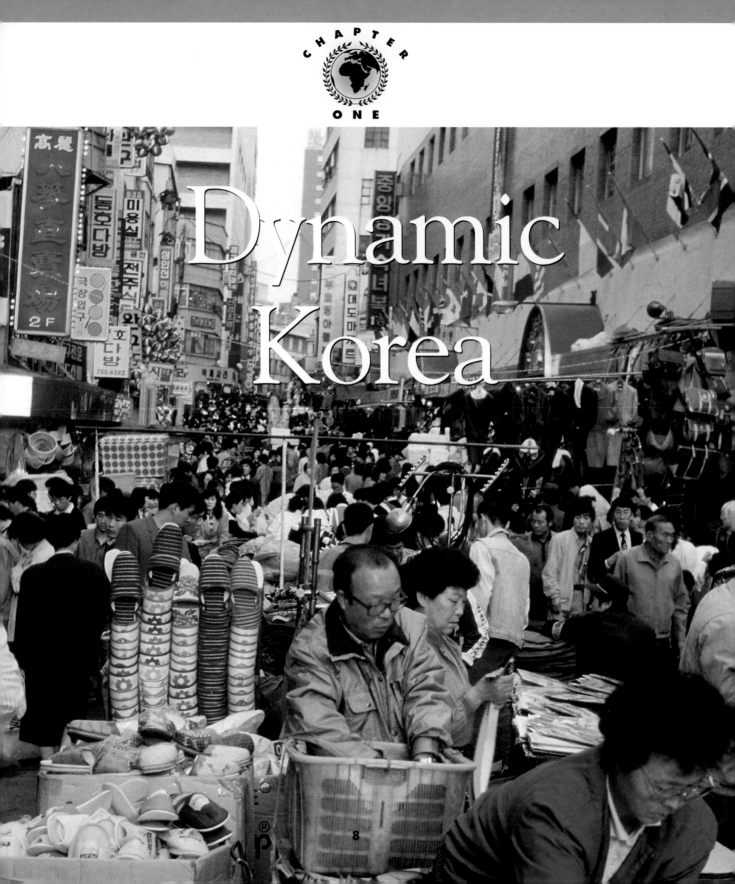

CHAPTER ONE

Dynamic Korea

SOUTH KOREA'S MOTTO IS "DYNAMIC KOREA." THE MOTTO expresses the pride that the people of South Korea have for their nation's prosperous economy and successful democracy. Note that the phrase is "Dynamic Korea," not "Dynamic South Korea." The country's official name is the Republic of Korea (ROK), but its citizens refer to it simply as Korea. Other people and governments around the world refer to the ROK as South Korea. This distinguishes it from the Korean Peninsula's other country—the Democratic People's Republic of Korea (DPRK). The DPRK is called North Korea by the rest of the world.

Opposite: **Shoppers crowd the streets around Namdaemun Market in Seoul.**

A busy street in Busan

A North Korean train crosses the DMZ into South Korea. In 2007, trains traveled the tracks between North Korea and South Korea for the first time in more than fifty years.

Two Nations, One Peninsula

For most of history, South Korea and North Korea were part of the same nation or colony. Since the end of World War II in 1945, the Korean Peninsula has been divided almost in half. In 1948, the ROK and the DPRK officially declared their independence and set up their own governments. Then, from 1950 to 1953, the two countries fought a war. At the end of the war, the border between North Korea and South Korea was closed, and a Demilitarized Zone (DMZ) was created. The DMZ is a strip of land that runs all the way across the peninsula, serving as a buffer between the two countries. The division of Korea split up families. North Koreans and South Koreans are kept apart.

Since the end of the Korean War, the two Koreas have gone down different roads in almost all aspects of life. After some early political violence and assassinations, South Korea has gradually become a democratic republic with

What Is Korea?

In this book, the term *Korea* refers to the Korean Peninsula and to the nation or colony of Korea before 1945. The peninsula was divided in 1945, and two independent countries were established in 1948. In this book, we refer to the Democratic People's Republic of Korea (DPRK) as North Korea, and the Republic of Korea (ROK) as South Korea.

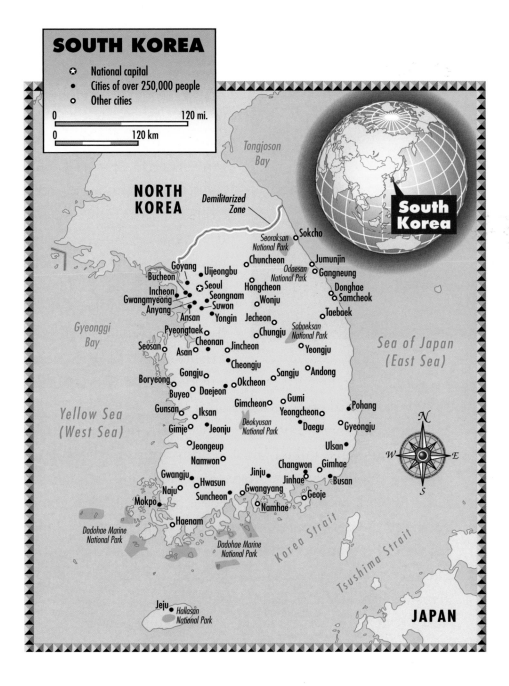

SOUTH KOREA

- ✪ National capital
- ● Cities of over 250,000 people
- ○ Other cities

0   120 mi.

0   120 km

Tongjoson Bay

NORTH KOREA

South Korea

Demilitarized Zone

Seoraksan National Park   Sokcho

Chuncheon   Jumunjin

Odaesan National Park   Gangneung

Goyang   Uijeongbu

Bucheon

Hongcheon

Incheon   Seongnam   Donghae

Gwangmyeong   Suwon   Wonju   Samcheok

Anyang

Ansan   Yongin   Jecheon   Taebaek

Pyeongtaek   Chungju

Gyeonggi Bay

Sabaeksan National Park

Seosan   Cheonan   Jincheon   Yeongju

Asan

Cheongju

Gongju   Sangju   Andong

Boryeong   Okcheon

Buyeo   Daejeon

Gunsan   Gimcheon   Gumi

Iksan   Yeongcheon   Pohang

Yellow Sea (West Sea)

Gimje   Jeonju   Daegu   Gyeongju

Deokyusan National Park

Jeongeup   Ulsan

Namwon   Changwon   Gimhae

Gwangju   Jinju   Jinhae   Busan

Naju   Hwasun

Gwangyang   Geoje

Mokpo   Suncheon

Namhae

Haenam

Sea of Japan (East Sea)

Dadohae Marine National Park

Dadohae Marine National Park

Korea Strait

Tsushima Strait

Jeju

Hallasan National Park

JAPAN

many political parties. North Korea, however, is a dictator-ship. It has had only two leaders in its history. The economies and societies of the two countries are also quite different.

Farmers harvesting a field of rice. Rice is South Korea's most valuable crop.

South Korea's economy is flourishing. It has strong manufacturing and agriculture sectors. North Korea's economy remains totally controlled by the government. It emphasizes building heavy machinery to support a large military. Farming is difficult in North Korea because of the cold climate and poor irrigation. And North Korea has very little trade with other countries, while South Korea's economy depends on international trade.

Despite the many differences between the two Koreas, their governments have talked about reunification. Little progress has been made, however. Many Koreans think it might be better to work on bringing the people of Korea back together instead of the governments. If the border was reopened, families could be reunited, and trade between the two countries could expand. Since 2000, some progress has been made. Many South Koreans have traveled to North Korea, but North Koreans are still not free to leave their country.

Korean Spelling

In 2000, South Korea's government changed the way written Korean is spelled when using the Latin alphabet, which is the alphabet of English. For example, the city name *Pusan* is now written *Busan*; *Taegu* is now spelled *Daegu*; and *Cheju* Island is now *Jeju* Island. In this book, the new spellings are used.

Nicknames Tell Korea's Story

Throughout their five-thousand-year history, the Korean people have had a variety of names for their land. Perhaps the best-known name is Joseon, which means "Land of the Morning Calm." This name comes from the peaceful look of the land in the morning. At that time of day, mist often hangs over the mountains, giving the land a dreamlike quality.

The history of the Korean Peninsula has hardly been calm, however. Over the centuries, armies from China, Mongolia, Manchuria, and Japan have tried to conquer the Korean people.

Mist shrouds the mountains near Gyeongju.

Even during hard times, the Korean people maintained their spirit and held on to their culture. To this day, Koreans have not mixed much with other people. Although intermarriage between Koreans and people of other ethnic backgrounds is more common than it once was, it is still rare. In addition, Koreans have continued to speak their own language, play their traditional games, and cook their traditional foods.

The Korean people were also sometimes known among their neighbors as "the Courteous People of the East." This name came from the way Koreans treated one another and, especially, foreigners. Traditionally, Koreans followed a strict social code of conduct called Confucianism. Because of this code, everyone knew exactly what was expected of them. They knew where they stood in relationship to everyone else. Korean courtesy extends to foreigners and to other Koreans in the same way today.

For many years, South Korea was called "the Miracle on the Han River." This referred to the way South Korea's government and people had rebuilt the country since the 1960s. South Korea went from a poor, farming

A South Korean family enjoys a meal together.

country to a rich, industrial country. Today, it has the eleventh-largest economy among the nations of the world. In many other ways, South Korea is thriving. South Korean students have higher average test scores than students in many other countries. South Korea has opened its doors to trade, sports competitions, and cultural events. It hosted the Summer Olympics in 1988 and co-hosted soccer's World Cup in 2002. Each year, South Korea holds fashion fairs and film festivals that draw people from around the world. In recent years, South Korea's popular culture—music, TV shows, and films—has washed over Asia in what is called "the Korean Wave." "Dynamic Korea" is playing an ever more prominent role in Asia and around the world.

In 2002, South Korea and Japan hosted the World Cup, the biggest tournament in soccer. The South Korean team made it to the semifinals.

The Natural Landscape

SOUTH KOREA SPREADS OUT OVER THE SOUTHERN HALF of the Korean Peninsula. It covers 38,022 square miles (98,477 square kilometers), which makes it a bit larger than the state of Indiana. To the west, the Yellow Sea, which Koreans call the West Sea, separates South Korea from eastern China. The Sea of Japan, which Koreans call the East Sea, lies to the east. To the south is the Korea Strait, which separates South Korea from Japan. South Korea's northern border lies within the Demilitarized Zone (DMZ), which divides North Korea from South Korea. The DMZ is a strip of land about 2.5 miles (4 km) wide that runs across the entire peninsula.

Opposite: **Jagged rocks rise from the Sea of Japan (East Sea) in eastern South Korea.**

South Korea's long coastline is a mix of sandy beaches and steep cliffs.

A Mountainous Land

Mountains rise over about 70 percent of South Korea. The Central Mountains region covers eastern and central South Korea and includes two main mountain ranges, the Taebaek and the Sobaek. The Taebaek Range runs northwest to southeast before it plunges steeply into the Sea of Japan. Along this rugged seacoast are several short stretches of sandy beaches and many protected harbors. The tallest peak in the Taebaek Range is Seoraksan, which reaches 5,604 feet (1,708 meters) above sea level. *San* means "mountain" in Korean.

Seoraksan, a peak in eastern South Korea, is famed for its beautiful fall colors.

The Taebaek Range is the source of South Korea's longest rivers—the Nakdong and the Han. The Nakdong winds its way south, emptying into the Sea of Japan at Busan. The Han flows northwest into the Yellow Sea at Seoul.

Farther inland, the Sobaek Range forms an S through the middle of the country. Jirisan is the highest peak in this range, standing 6,283 feet (1,915 m) above sea level. Other high peaks include Sobaeksan, Woraksan, Songnisan, and Gayasan. These peaks are the centerpieces of some of South Korea's national parks.

Many of South Korea's largest lakes are in this mountainous central region, including Lake Soyang, South Korea's largest lake. The lakes were formed by damming rivers.

Both the Taebaek and the Sobaek ranges are heavily forested. Some small valleys and areas along the coast are used to grow crops.

The Han is a broad river. In Seoul, it is more than half a mile (1 km) wide.

South Korea's Geographic Features

Area: 38,022 square miles (98,477 sq km)

Highest Elevation: Hallasan, 6,398 feet (1,950 m) above sea level

Lowest Elevation: Sea level along the coast

Longest River: Nakdong River, 324 miles (521 km) long

Largest Lake: Lake Soyang, 329 miles (530 km) long, 404 feet (123 m) deep

Largest Island: Jeju Island, 700 square miles (1,800 sq km)

Coastline: 1,499 miles (2,413 km)

Greatest Distance North to South: 300 miles (480 km)

Greatest Distance East to West: 185 miles (298 km)

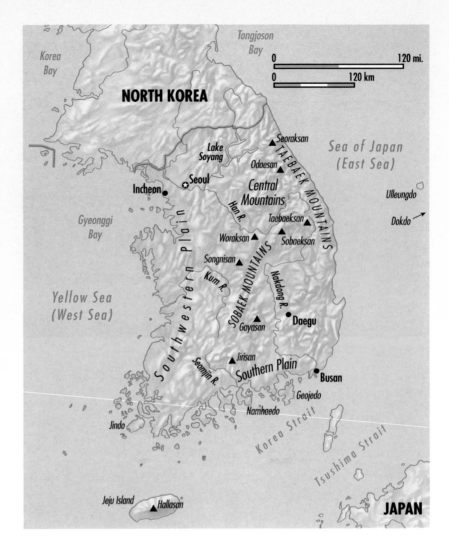

Lowlands and Plains

Plains, lowlands, and low hills cover most of western South Korea. Several long rivers and many short, fast-flowing streams race down the mountains and across the plains. The Southwestern Plain stretches all along South Korea's western coast. This region is an important farming area in South Korea. Several large cities are also on this plain, including Seoul—

South Korea's capital and largest city—and Incheon. More than half of all South Koreans live on the Southwestern Plain.

Seoul is a large city filled with modern skyscrapers.

The Southern Plain blankets the southern tip of the Korean Peninsula. Inland, this region is filled with rich farmland. Along the coast, many inlets and bays cut into the land. Two of South Korea's largest cities, Busan and Daegu, are located on the Southern Plain.

Taking a Mud Bath

A unique spot on South Korea's western coast is Daecheon Beach, near Boryeong City. The sandy beach was formed from shells pulverized by the ocean's surf. Nearby are mudflats. Mud from this spot is made into cosmetics, and many visitors to the area come to bathe in the mud or receive mud massages. They then rinse off in the sea.

Every July, Boryeong holds the Mud Festival. Activities include mud slides, mud wrestling matches, and the crowning of a mud king. At night during the festival, fireworks light up the beach.

More than a thousand islands lie off the South Korean coast. The word *do* means "island" in Korean and appears in many island names. Ulleungdo and Dokdo, which are in the Sea of Japan, are the easternmost points of South Korea. Both islands were formed by volcanoes. They have steep cliffs that plunge to the sea. Although Japan also claims Dokdo, the island is under South Korean control. Geojedo and Namhaedo lie just off the coast south of Busan. Both islands have beautiful beaches. Geojedo is known for the Haegeumgang Rocks, sheer cliffs that rise from the sea. Namhaedo is best known for the impressive suspension bridge that connects it to the mainland. The bridge is 2,165 feet (660 m) long.

Ulleungdo lies about 75 miles (120 km) east of the Korean mainland. About ten thousand people live on the rocky, steep-sided island.

A Look at South Korea's Cities

Busan (below), located at the mouth of the Nakdong River on the southeast coast, is the second-largest city in South Korea after the capital, Seoul, and the largest seaport. Busan is also a major industrial center. Shipbuilding, car-making, electronics, and textiles are the main industries. Its beaches and hot springs draw many tourists. Busan has one of the mildest climates on the Korean Peninsula, though heavy summer rains fall and an occasional typhoon blows through.

Incheon, another major port and industrial center, is South Korea's third-largest city. It lies in the northwest, on the Yellow Sea. Incheon is South Korea's main entry point by air. Its principal industries include making iron, steel, and glass; information technology; and traditional ceramics. Both visitors and residents enjoy the Songdo Amusement Park.

South Korea's fourth-largest city is Daegu. Located northwest of Busan, Daegu sits on a large plain surrounded by mountains. Attractions range from the Donghwasa Buddhist Temple (above), built in A.D. 493, to the modern Culture and Arts Center that opened in 1991. Daegu is also known as the textile and fashion center of South Korea. Every May and October, the city hosts the Daegu Textile Fashion Festival, which draws buyers from around the world.

Azaleas blanket the ground on Jeju Island near Hallasan. Many people visit Jeju to enjoy its stunning scenery.

South Korea's largest island is Jeju, which sits off the peninsula's southwestern tip. The island was formed by volcanic eruptions. Even today, volcanic rock and clay cover the ground. Hallasan, a dormant volcano in the middle of Jeju Island, is South Korea's highest peak. At the top is a crater filled with water, called Baekrokdam Lake.

Another volcanic peak, Seongsan Ilchulbong, is on the northwestern end of Jeju Island. Its name means "Sunrise Peak." It earned this name because in the morning, the rising sun makes the nearby seawater look red.

Four Seasons

South Korea has four definite seasons: winter, spring, summer, and fall. Winter starts in December and ends in mid-March. Cold, dry winds blow down the peninsula from northern Asia. January is the coldest month, with average temperatures below freezing. Winter also brings heavy snowfall, especially in the mountains of the north and east. The winters along the southern coast and on Jeju Island are warmer.

In early spring, yellow dust and sand blow down the Korean Peninsula from China's deserts. By mid-April, South Korea

Typhoon Maemi

In late summer or early fall, two or three typhoons usually hit southeastern Korea. Typhoons are violent storms that develop over the warm waters of the western Pacific Ocean. Their strong winds and heavy rains can be devastating when they hit land.

On September 12, 2003, Typhoon Maemi blew through southeastern Korea with winds that reached 135 miles per hour (217 kph). These were the strongest winds ever recorded in Korea. The storm damaged rice crops, blew down giant cranes, sank oil tankers, washed out railroad tracks, and destroyed about 2,500 houses. The typhoon caused an estimated US$4.1 billion in damage. It is thought to have killed 115 people, at least 85 of them in South Korea.

begins to warm up. Farmers plant their crops and prepare the fields to grow rice. Flowers cover the fields and mountains, and cherry blossoms add to the springtime colors.

Summer begins in June and ends in early September. This is South Korea's wettest season. Winds called monsoons draw warm, wet air from the southeastern Pacific Ocean over the land. The heaviest rains fall in the far south. August is the hottest, most humid month. During this time of year, the air is sometimes so humid that clothes hanging on a line take days to dry.

Most South Koreans agree that fall is the best season. By then, the heavy summer rains have ended. The temperatures have cooled a bit, and everything is less sticky. In fall, the landscape turns from greens to brilliant yellows, oranges, and reds as the leaves change color.

Cherry trees in Seoul burst into bloom in April.

Plants and Animals

SOUTH KOREANS TAKE GREAT PRIDE IN THEIR NATURAL environment. Homes, public buildings, and cities are planned with the environment in mind. Houses and other structures are often built facing water, such as a river or the ocean, to catch warm air in winter or cool breezes in summer. Buildings and cities are also built with a mountain at their back to protect them from cold winds. Within homes, buildings, and cities, relaxing garden areas are set aside.

Opposite: **Snow blankets the trees high in the mountains of South Korea.**

Visitors admire miniature trees in a garden on Jeju Island.

About 4,500 different kinds of plants grow in South Korea, including about 160 native tree species. Forests cover about two-thirds of South Korea, mostly in mountainous areas. Many kinds of pine trees, including spruce, larch, cedar, and Siberian fir, grace the mountain slopes. Pine trees have long been important in Korean art and folklore. They are admired for their color, form, and fragrance. Pine leaves and nuts are the main source of food for many birds and wild animals.

The willow and the birch are also important in South Korea. To Koreans, the willow symbolizes peace and beauty. Birch trees supply some of South Korea's hardest wood, which is made into tool handles. Many altars in temples are also made of birch. Other hardwood trees found throughout South Korea include beech, elm, and gingko. Broadleaf trees stand along the southern coast and on Jeju Island.

Dense forests cover many mountains in South Korea.

The bamboo plant has been important throughout Korean history. It rises straight and tall in wetlands. Long ago, bamboo symbolized the pure spirit of Korean scholars. Bamboo today is a symbol of strength and of long life. Its straight, graceful form appears in many Korean paintings. Bamboo is strong, flexible, and light. It is used to make everything from musical instruments to rugs to flooring.

An important plant, which grows underground, is the ginseng plant. Its roots are believed to improve strength and health. Koreans use it in foods, chewing gum, drinks, and medicines. Ginseng root is now grown commercially, but the most powerful roots still grow in the wild.

Many kinds of flowering plants bloom in South Korea. Azaleas, gentians, and rhododendrons grow in the mountains. Cosmos, chrysanthemums, dianthuses, fuchsias, and lilies brighten meadows. Lotus blossoms float on ponds. Jeju Hanran orchids and Halla Songi plants are found only on Jeju Island.

Images of bamboo have long appeared in Korean art. This vase dates back eight hundred years.

Blooming with Courage

South Korea's national flower is the rose of Sharon, a white hibiscus with a rose-colored center. In Korean, the flower is called the *mugunghwa* because it symbolizes *mugung*, or "immortality." Its delicate blooms survive even in harsh weather. The rose of Sharon represents the Koreans' courage, which Koreans credit with helping them survive hardship.

Asiatic black bears were once common in the mountains of South Korea. Today, only about ten bears still live in the wild in South Korea.

Wildlife

At one time, antelope, bears, leopards, lynx, and Siberian tigers roamed South Korean's forests and mountains. Most scientists believe the great cats no longer survive there. In recent years, a few bears have been spotted in the mountains of northern South Korea. Today, the largest common animals in South Korea are wild boars, deer, and wolves. Smaller mammals found in South Korea include badgers, foxes, martens, pikas, water shrews, muskrats, and weasels.

South Korea also has some unusual animals. The Amur goral, a white antelope with small, cone-shaped horns, is now endangered. Ponies run wild on Jeju Island. Their ancestors were left behind by Mongolian invaders in the early 1300s. In 2003, scientists found a new species of salamander in the woods of South Korea. The Korean lungless crevice salamander absorbs oxygen directly through its moist skin rather than through lungs.

More than four hundred kinds of birds have been seen in South Korea. Some live in the country year-round, while many

The discovery of the Korean lungless crevice salamander in 2003 startled scientists. Although many species of lungless salamanders live in the Americas, this was the first one discovered in Asia.

Elegant red-crowned cranes stand about 5 feet (1.5 m) high.

more pass through on their annual migration. These include swans, cormorants, black-faced spoonbills, white-tailed sea eagles, and blackhead gulls. Herons, cranes, and other waterbirds nest along the coastline and in rice paddies. Game birds include ducks, geese, and ring-necked pheasants. Among the nation's endangered birds are the Manchurian crane and Tristram's woodpecker.

South Korea's coastal waters teem with life. Large creatures found in Korean waters include sharks, squid, and octopuses. Shellfish such as abalones, clams, oysters, scallops, and shrimps are common. Pearl-producing oysters are found along the southern coast. Pollack, filefish, and sardines are just a few of the many fish found along the coast. Carps, eels, smelts, and trout swim in South Korea's lakes.

The Jindo Dog

Although South Korea does not have a national animal, the South Korean government named the Jindo dog a "natural monument." The Jindo dog is native to a large island in the southwest of the country called Jindo. It has white or yellow fur; short, pointed ears; a thick neck; and a bushy, curly tail. The Jindo dog is renowned for its fierce loyalty and bravery.

National Parks and Gardens

Korea has a long tradition of protecting the environment. Conservation laws were passed as early as the A.D. 500s. For centuries, monks guarded the natural areas around their monasteries. Today, many of South Korea's national parks are on the sites of these ancient monasteries. South Korea has at least twenty national parks and about the same number of provincial parks. South Korea's oldest and largest trees are found in these protected areas.

South Korea is mountainous, so most of the protected areas are centered on well-known peaks. Seoraksan National Park stands in northeastern South Korea. Many people consider it South Korea's most rugged and beautiful national park. It attracts more than three million visitors each year. They come

Seoraksan is South Korea's most popular national park. It is famous for its misty mountains, dramatic waterfalls, and colorful fall leaves.

The DMZ: An Accidental Nature Preserve

Perhaps the only good thing to come out of the Korean War is an accidental nature preserve that developed in the Demilitarized Zone. Since 1953, barbed wire has enclosed this stretch of land between North Korea and South Korea, keeping people out. As a result, the DMZ became a haven for endangered and rare animals. Amur leopards, Asiatic black bears, Eurasian lynx, and Amur gorals live in the DMZ. Some scientists think they have found footprints of Siberian tigers. Migratory birds such as black-faced spoonbills, red-crowned cranes, and white-naped cranes winter in the DMZ.

The two Koreas are working to increase trade and tourism, and two railroad lines and two highways now cross the DMZ. Environmentalists fear that more development in the DMZ will threaten the area's rare plant and animal life.

Anapji Pond was built as part of the palace complex of the ancient kingdom of Silla.

to admire the jagged peaks, enjoy walks in the thick forests of broadleaf and pine trees, and perhaps see some deer or bears.

Dadohae Marine National Park is the country's largest park, covering about 1,700 islands off the southern coast. Hongdo is among the most visited islands. It is famous for its deep ravines, steep cliffs, diverse plant and animal life, and brilliant sunsets.

In South Korea's national parks, the natural environment is protected. South Korea's many gardens also look like natural areas, but people had to work hard to make them appear this way. In fact, South Koreans want their gardens to look more natural than nature. The basic elements of a South Korean garden include water, rocks, wood, and plants. Koreans can trace their interest in gardens back to about 30 B.C. The best-preserved of Korea's early gardens is Anapji Pond in Gyeongju. It was made in about A.D. 670. Large rocks line the bank of the pond. Wooden pavilions share the shoreline with rows of willow trees.

One of South Korea's newer gardens is the Yeomiji Botanical Garden on the southwestern coast of Jeju Island. About two thousand kinds of plants are arranged in traditional Korean gardens as well as in Japanese, French, and Italian styles.

Seoul's Recovered Stream

The Cheonggye Stream flows through Seoul. Between 1958 and 1961, it was paved over to build an expressway. By the first years of the twenty-first century, the mayor of Seoul, Lee Myung-bak, decided to bring more nature to the city. A project began to uncover and restore the stream. In 2005, the stream officially reopened. For the first time in decades, the people of Seoul could watch water tumble over rocks and gravel. Today, twenty-two bridges cross the Cheonggye. The stream includes a waterfall and an area where people can wade into the water.

Five Thousand Years of History

36

PEOPLE WERE LIVING ON THE KOREAN PENINSULA AS EARLY as 28,000 B.C. Tools and pottery from these early people have been found near the present-day cities of Pyongyang in North Korea and Seoul and Busan in South Korea. In about 3000 B.C., people moved from the Altai Mountain area of central Asia onto the Korean Peninsula. They likely pushed the earlier people off the peninsula. Modern Koreans trace their ancestry and their spoken language to these central Asian migrants. For this reason, Koreans say that their history spans five thousand years.

Opposite: **Cheomseongdae, an astronomical observatory, was built in 647. It is one of the oldest structures in Korea.**

Dangun: The Legendary Founder of Korea

According to legend, Dangun is the founder of Korea and the father of the Korean people. His father was Hwanung, the son of the ruler of heaven. His mother was a woman who had been a bear until Hwanung transformed her. The legend says that Dangun was born near Mount Baekdu in what is now North Korea. In 2333 B.C., Dangun is said to have moved to Pyongyang, where he built a walled city and established the Ancient Joseon Kingdom. Dangun is supposed to have lived more than a thousand years before he became a mountain god in far northern Korea. Today, Koreans celebrate October 3 as National Foundation Day. On that day in 2333 B.C., Dangun supposedly founded Ancient Joseon.

Ancient Joseon and Chinese Influence

The early Koreans hunted, fished, and gathered food. Later, they began to farm. In time, they founded the Ancient Joseon Kingdom. Ancient Joseon was probably located between the Liao River in southern Manchuria, in what is now China, and the Daedong River in what is now North Korea. Large clans built walled towns in Ancient Joseon. The kingdom's warriors used bronze and iron daggers and spears. Farmers had iron hoes, plowshares, and sickles. These tools helped them increase their rice crop production.

Ancient Joseon had close contact with China, but China did not consider Ancient Joseon an equal, independent country. In 109 B.C., the emperor of China's Han dynasty decided to expand his empire and attacked Ancient Joseon. The following year, the Joseon capital, Asadal, fell to the Han. China set up four territories. Each territory sent yearly tribute to China in the form of crops and other goods. In exchange for the tribute, China protected the territories from invaders. Over the course of several hundred years, this contact with China brought three important influences to Korea: the Chinese written language, Buddhism, and Confucianism. Because the Koreans had no written language, they used the Chinese writing system. Buddhism

These covered cups date to Korea's Three Kingdoms period. They were probably used in ceremonies.

eventually became the dominant religion on the peninsula. The Confucian code for organizing society and government enabled Korea's rulers to maintain order.

The Three Kingdoms

Little by little, China lost direct control of the four Korean territories. By 57 B.C., the people in the northern part of the peninsula had been unified as the Goguryeo Kingdom. About this time, two kingdoms were formed in the southern part of the peninsula: Silla and Baekje. Goguryeo, Silla, and Baekje are known as the Three Kingdoms.

During the A.D. 300s, Goguryeo adopted Buddhism and established a Confucian academy. In 384, Baekje adopted Buddhism. By the 500s, the other two kingdoms also adopted Buddhism and Confucianism. Silla made its own advances in science and technology. During the mid-600s, Cheomseongdae, one of the first astronomical observatories in East Asia, was built in the Silla capital at Gyeongju. The world's first woodblock printing also occurred there.

The Three Kingdoms and Unified Silla

Three Kingdoms, ca. 57 B.C.–A.D. 668
Unified Silla, 668–918
Present-day boundary

Bulguksa Temple was built in 744. Its wooden shrines are located on the slopes of Tohamsan in the southeast of the country.

Unified Silla

All three kingdoms sent tribute to China. They also fought with one another. Eventually, Silla formed an alliance with China's Tang dynasty. With Tang help, Silla conquered Baekje in 660 and Goguryeo in 668, unifying much of the Korean Peninsula.

For 250 years, Unified Silla controlled the Korean Peninsula from Pyongyang to the southern tip. The kings of Silla set up a strict social and political order for wealthy families called the bone-rank system. A person's or a family's bone rank determined their home's size; their clothing type and color; and the number of horses, carriages, and other goods they could own.

Most peasant farmers owned their land. Their main crops were rice and hemp. Farmers paid taxes and had to perform free labor for the government. They built roads and irrigation canals as part of this labor.

During the 700s, the Silla dynasty reached the height of its power and wealth. The great Buddhist temple Bulguksa and the Seokguram Grotto were built during this period. Korea's largest bronze temple bells were also cast in these years. Korea's temple bells have a unique dome shape. The largest one is the Emille Bell. It is 12 feet (3.6 m) high and measures 7.3 feet (2.2 m) across at the bottom.

In the 800s, Silla began to break apart. Aristocrats began to chip away at the king's powers. Peasants who were treated unfairly rebelled.

The Emille Bell hangs in Gyeongju. Locals say its sound can be heard 30 miles (50 km) away.

The Goryeo Dynasty

In 918, a general named Wang Kon established a new dynasty, with its capital at Gaeseong. He called it Goryeo. The name *Korea* comes from this dynasty's name. In 935, Wang received a formal surrender from the last Silla king. He also married a woman from the Silla royal family. Wang reunited the peninsula and extended the northern border to the mouth of the Yalu River. In 1044, a later Goryeo ruler had a great wall built from the Yalu southeast to the Sea of Japan.

Goryeo kings brought Confucian scholars into the government. Knowledge rather than rank became important as a way to advance oneself. Koreans had many cultural achievements under the Goryeo. They developed inlaid designs in a special kind of pottery known as celadon. They printed the entire works of Buddhist teaching using more than eighty-one thousand woodblocks. In 1234, they used the world's first movable metal type.

Delicate Korean celadon pottery developed during the Goryeo dynasty. Korean celadon is usually a pale blue-green.

In 1231, the Mongols, a people from central Asia, invaded the Korean Peninsula. This was the beginning of the end of the Goryeo dynasty. The Mongols conquered China, establishing the Yuan dynasty there. Then, in 1259, they completed their conquest of Korea.

Korea's social structure fell apart under the Mongols. Korean aristocrats gained control of farmland. Peasant farmers became serfs, who no longer owned the land. They had to do the landowners' bidding. Artisans and other middle-class people became slaves. Some of these people, along with ginseng, horses, gold, and silver, were given in tribute to the Mongols. Finally, in the 1350s, the Goryeo king was able to push the Mongols out of Korea.

This Buddhist painting was created in the thirteenth century, during the Goryeo dynasty.

Korean Governments

Ancient Joseon Kingdom	Prior to 108 B.C.
The Three Kingdoms	About 57 B.C.–A.D. 668
Unified Silla	668–918
Goryeo dynasty	918–1392
Joseon dynasty	1392–1910
Colony of Japan	1910–1945
Temporary division of the peninsula	1945–1948
Democratic People's Republic of Korea (North Korea)	1948–present
Republic of Korea (South Korea)	1948–present

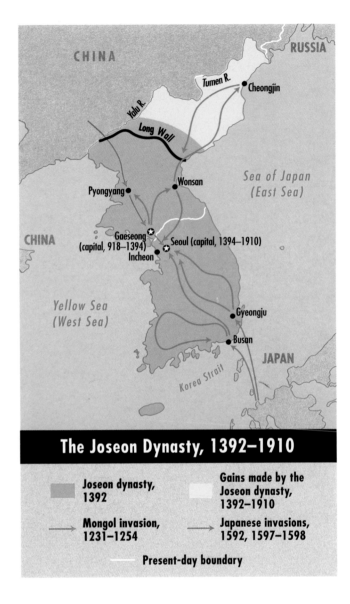

The Joseon Dynasty, 1392–1910

▨ Joseon dynasty, 1392	▨ Gains made by the Joseon dynasty, 1392–1910
→ Mongol invasion, 1231–1254	→ Japanese invasions, 1592, 1597–1598
— Present-day boundary	

With the Mongols gone and Korea in a state of decay, General Yi Song-gye seized power. In 1392, Yi was proclaimed king and established the Joseon dynasty. He moved the capital to Seoul and began construction of a wall around the city. Yi replaced Buddhism with Confucianism as the state religion. Yi placed all Korean land under his own control. He parceled the land out to military leaders and government officials.

Yi's grandson, Sejong, reigned as king from 1418 to 1450. He is regarded as Korea's greatest ruler. Sejong extended the Korean border in the north to the Yalu and Tumen rivers, and that remains North Korea's northern border today. He encouraged inventions, such as the rain gauge. A Korean alphabet called *hangeul* was also invented during his rule. Unfortunately, the Confucian system that Sejong and later Joseon kings promoted created a strict social system with little chance for advancement. It also discouraged the development of industry and trade.

In 1592, the Japanese began a campaign to attack the Ming dynasty in China by going through Korea. They landed at

Busan and then captured Seoul and most of the peninsula. The Ming Chinese and armies of Korean landowners, peasants, and slaves united to force the Japanese out. A second unsuccessful attack by Japan began in 1597. The attacks, however, greatly weakened Korea and its government. Thousands of people died, land was destroyed, fewer crops were grown, and the amount of taxes the government was able to collect decreased.

Korea recovered from the Japanese invasions, but then the Manchus of Manchuria invaded from the north in 1627 and 1636. The Joseon dynasty surrendered after the Manchus killed many Koreans and devastated the land. Korea then sent tribute to the Manchus. In 1644, the Manchus overthrew the Ming dynasty in China and set up the Qing dynasty. In

Turtle Ships

During the Japanese invasion in 1592, Korean admiral Yi Sun-sin (1545–1598) developed the world's first ironclad ships. They were called turtle ships because of their protective metal shell. Spears and arrows simply bounced off the ironclad ships. Though Yi had only a few ironclad ships, they destroyed hundreds of Japanese supply ships in the Korea Strait. This helped save Korea. In 1597, the Japanese attacked again, and once more Yi's navy defeated them. Yi was killed during one of the battles, however. Today, Yi Sun-sin is considered one of Korea's great heroes. A festival is held in his honor every spring.

response to the Japanese and Manchu invasions, the Joseon dynasty closed off Korea to all countries except China. The kings built a high wooden fence across Korea's northern border. Korea became known as the "Hermit Kingdom."

Between the 1640s and 1876, Korea remained isolated from the rest of the world. Korean officials, however, sometimes met Western scholars in China. These officials brought back books about the Catholic religion. They also brought back inventions such as telescopes and alarm clocks. At the same time in Korea, a group of scholars were promoting *sirhak*, or "practical learning." These scholars were critical of parts of Confucianism's strict social code. Instead, they promoted social equality and the welfare of all people. They also believed that the educated should work to improve agriculture.

Korea began trading with foreign countries in the late 1800s. This painting shows Japanese military officers (right) meeting with Korean officials.

Busan was one of the first Korean ports opened to Japanese trade. Today, it is the second-largest city in South Korea.

Foreigners Arrive

In 1876, Japan forced the Joseon dynasty to open Korea's doors. That year, Korea opened the ports of Busan, Incheon, and Wonsan to Japanese trade. In 1882, the United States and Korea signed a treaty establishing trade and diplomatic relations. Within the next few years, France, Germany, Great Britain, Italy, and Russia also signed treaties with Korea. Government representatives, businesspeople, and religious missionaries from those countries came to Korea. Groups from Japan and the Western countries worked to make doing business in Korea easier. They built Korea's first railroads. Telegraph and telephone lines connected Korea's main cities. Missionaries worked to make life better for the Korean people. They built hospitals, schools, and universities.

By the end of the 1800s, the Joseon dynasty was weak. Korea's neighbors—China, Japan, and Russia—tried to gain control of the peninsula. In 1894 and 1895, Japan fought China

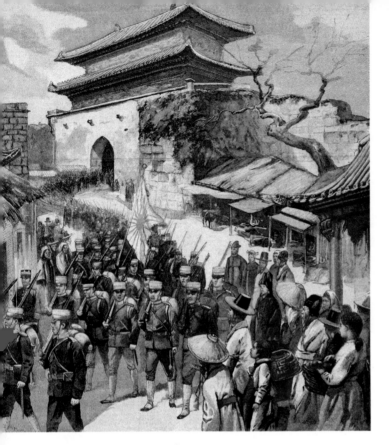

Japanese soldiers march into Seoul in 1904. Japanese soldiers would occupy Korea for another forty-one years.

for influence in Korea. Japan won the war and forced China to recognize Korea as an independent country. Korea no longer had to pay tribute to China. Then, in 1904 and 1905, Japan and Russia fought for control of Korea. Again, Japan won the war. Russia recognized Japan's influence over Korea. In 1910, Japan forced King Sunjong, the last Joseon king, to sign a treaty that made Korea a colony of Japan. Korea was no longer independent.

Japan Rules Korea

From 1910 to 1945, Japan ruled Korea as a colony. This meant that Korea and its people existed for the benefit of Japan. Many Japanese farmers and fishers came to work in Korea. They were given Korean farmland and rights to fish in Korean waters.

Japan began a program to strip Koreans of their national identity. Japan wanted the Koreans to become like the Japanese, although Koreans could not become Japanese citizens. The Korean spoken and written language was replaced with Japanese. Korean language and history were no longer taught in schools. Later, the Japanese even forced the Korean people to replace their Korean names with Japanese ones. In reaction to these policies, thousands of Koreans left their homeland and migrated to China, Russia, and the Hawaiian Islands.

Many Koreans struggled against Japanese control. On March 1, 1919, Korean nationalists signed a declaration of independence that was read in the streets of Seoul, Pyongyang, and other cities. For several weeks, thousands of people throughout Korea took part in peaceful demonstrations for independence from Japan. The Japanese put down this movement and killed about seven thousand Koreans. As a result, Korean nationalists fled to Shanghai, China, or to the newly formed communist Soviet Union, which had been known as Russia until 1917. In Shanghai, the nationalists set up the Provisional Government of the Republic of Korea. Syngman Rhee was elected president of this government in exile.

Japanese police officers in Korea. The number of Japanese in Korea peaked at more than six hundred thousand in the 1940s.

In the 1930s, Japan used Korea as a staging area for its invasion of Manchuria and then of China. Korean crops fed the Japanese army. Korean boys and men were forced to serve in the Japanese army. Other Koreans were taken to Japan to work on farms or in factories. Only in recent years has it come to light that tens of thousands of Korean women were forced to act as prostitutes for the Japanese army. Many of them died of malnutrition and disease. Those who survived lived in shame for years. Because of the hardships the Korean people endured during the time of Japanese rule, many Koreans still harbor harsh feelings toward Japan.

In 1939, World War II broke out in Europe. Before this war started, Japan had formed an alliance with Germany and Italy. These countries were known as the Axis Powers. Great Britain, France, and the Soviet Union, known as the Allies, opposed the Axis powers. In 1941, the United States joined the Allies when Japan attacked Pearl Harbor in the Hawaiian Islands.

The Japanese attack on Pearl Harbor damaged or destroyed eight U.S. Navy battleships and nearly two hundred planes.

United Nations forces cross the 38th Parallel in 1950. The Korean War would continue for three more years.

A Divided Korea and the Korean War

World War II ended in 1945 after the United States dropped atomic bombs on Japan. The Allies had previously agreed to temporarily divide the Korean Peninsula at the 38th Parallel and govern it as a trusteeship. Soviet troops marched into northern Korea and accepted the surrender of Japanese troops there. The United States accepted the surrender of Japanese troops in southern Korea.

The Soviet Union immediately closed off Korea at the 38th Parallel. They placed Korean communists in positions of power. Kim Il Sung was elected secretary of the North Korean Communist Party. He became chairman of the provisional government in the north. The U.S. military ran the government in the south. In 1948, elections supervised by the United Nations (UN) were supposed to take place in the north and the south. The result was to be an elected national assembly for a united Korea. The Soviets, however, refused to allow UN officials into the north.

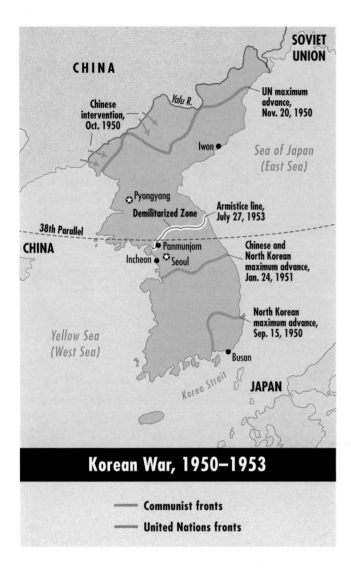

Korean War, 1950–1953

— Communist fronts
— United Nations fronts

In the south, voters elected a national assembly in May 1948. The national assembly wrote a constitution and formed a government. Syngman Rhee was elected president of South Korea in July 1948, and in August the Republic of Korea was proclaimed. In the north, the Supreme People's Assembly was formed. It appointed Kim Il Sung as premier, and soon the Democratic People's Republic of Korea was proclaimed in the north. In 1949, the Soviet Union and the United States withdrew their troops from the Korean Peninsula.

Then, in June 1950, Kim Il Sung began an invasion of South Korea. His goal was to reunify Korea under his control. The United States responded by having the UN organize troops from several countries. Within a few months, UN forces had pushed the North Korean army as far as the Yalu River. Kim soon received help from the Chinese communists, who had successfully taken over China the year before. About one million communist Chinese troops joined the North Koreans and drove the UN troops south of the 38th Parallel. A cease-fire was finally called in 1953. Though the fighting stopped, Korea remained divided at the 38th Parallel. A Demilitarized Zone (DMZ) was created across the middle of Korea. A peace treaty has never been signed to officially end the war.

When the fighting stopped in 1953, both North Korea and South Korea lay in ruins. Farmland had been trampled, forests had been destroyed, and railroads and highways had been torn up. Many cities had been flattened. Two million Koreans had been killed during the war. Millions more were homeless and jobless. Both countries had many years of rebuilding ahead of them.

Growth and Oppression

Syngman Rhee led South Korea until 1960. The government was weak and corrupt, and Rhee's time in office was marked by frequent student demonstrations. Rhee made few improvements to the economy, and South Korea's economic growth lagged behind that of North Korea. South Korea had few mineral deposits and had not been highly industrialized before the war. In 1960, it was still mainly a country of small farms. Finally, in 1960, Rhee stepped down and

Syngman Rhee resigned in 1960 in the face of large protests. He went into exile in Hawaii.

elections were held for a new government. The country's economic problems continued, however.

In May 1961, a military coup led by Park Chung-hee overthrew the government. During his years in power, Park led the country through a series of five-year economic plans. South Korea's economy boomed. The government built large highways and railroads to connect major cities. It nurtured a new auto industry as well as steel mills, cement plants, and shipbuilding factories. Park wanted to boost exports, so he encouraged manufacturers, both large and small, who produced all kinds of toys, shoes, clothes, and inexpensive electrical items. By the late 1970s, South Korea was known as the Miracle on the Han River.

Park Chung-hee is credited with turning South Korea into an economic powerhouse. The average per person income in South Korea increased tenfold during his time in office.

South Korea's economy boomed, but the country was not yet democratic. Park suppressed dissent, jailing many of his opponents. He had the South Korean Constitution rewritten to give himself unlimited power. Finally, even members of his own government had had enough. In 1979, the head of the country's National Security Force assassinated Park.

The next president, Choi Kyu-hah, was another military man. When the government delayed constitutional reforms, such as direct election of the president, many South Koreans

demonstrated in the streets. The most violent demonstra-tions were in the city of Gwangju. There, the military killed hundreds of demonstrators in what is known as the Gwangju Massacre. The incident caused Choi to resign. He was fol-lowed by former general Chun Doo-hwan.

While the economy continued to improve, South Koreans continued to demonstrate for a more democratic constitution. Finally, in October 1987, a new constitution was approved. It allowed for the direct election of the president. In December 1987, Roh Tae Woo, another former general, became the first directly elected president of South Korea. In 1992, Kim Young-sam became the first South Korean president with no ties to the military. Kim worked to rid the government of corruption.

After students began demonstrating for a more democratic government in 1980, the government banned political rallies and closed universities. When demonstrations continued, the government sent in troops.

Kim Dae-jung spent much of his long political career opposing South Korea's dictatorial leaders. He survived repeated arrests, a kidnapping, and an assassination attempt.

Into the Twenty-First Century

In 1997, Kim Dae-jung became South Korea's president. His rise to power had been a long struggle. He was imprisoned for six years for political reasons, faced death sentences five times, and spent ten years in exile or under house arrest. When Kim first gained power, South Korea was going through a financial crisis. He worked to restore South Korea's economy, which experienced rapid growth in 1999 and 2000. Kim is best known for his "Sunshine Policy" toward North Korea. In June 2000, that policy resulted in the first meeting ever held between the leaders of the two countries. The following December, Kim was awarded the Nobel Peace Prize for his work for democracy in South Korea and for reconciliation with North Korea. Later, it was revealed that Kim had agreed to pay the North Korean government $500,000 in U.S. dollars to have the June 2000 meeting.

In December 2002, Roh Moo-hyun, a political outsider, was elected president. Within a few months, his administration was rocked by a campaign fund-raising scandal. Roh's campaign had accepted illegal contributions. Roh almost resigned over the matter. Then, in March 2004, the National Assembly voted to impeach Roh for violating election laws during the 2004 elections. In May, the Constitutional Court overturned Roh's impeachment.

South Korea's economy grew during Roh's presidency, but many South Koreans thought the economy should be doing even better. By 2007, Roh had lost the support of the public and his own political party.

Still, Roh continued to work for closer relations with North Korea. In October 2007, Roh and Kim Jong Il, the leader of North Korea, held a summit. During the summit, Kim agreed to dismantle North Korea's nuclear weapons. Roh said that South Korea would provide aid for North Korea's industrial development. In addition, the North Korean and the South Korean leaders agreed to work toward a peace treaty that would finally, formally, end the Korean War.

A Young Democracy

OUTH KOREA'S CONSTITUTION GUARANTEES FREEDOM OF speech, press, and religion, and many other human and civil rights. For example, all citizens who are at least nineteen years old have the right to vote. South Koreans, however, have not always been able to exercise these rights. Elections were not free, with different political parties to choose from, until 1987. Before then, opponents of the government were often imprisoned or held under house arrest. Some left the country. South Korea's strong presidents rewrote the nation's constitution nine times. They gave themselves unlimited power and unlimited terms of office. In 1987, when the constitution was most recently rewritten, South Korea finally achieved true representative democracy. The 1987 constitution limits the powers of the president, strengthens the legislature, and protects human rights.

Opposite: **South Korean flags adorn the Seoul city hall on Liberation Day, which marks the end of Japanese rule in Korea.**

Student demonstrations were important in forcing South Korea to move toward democracy.

The Taegeukgi

South Korea's flag is called the *Taegeukgi* because of the *taegeuk* circle in the middle. The swirls in the circle represent the balance of forces in the universe. Red stands for positive forces, or *yang*. Blue stands for negative forces, or *eum*. The sets of lines in the corners of the flag also represent balance. The three unbroken lines in the top left corner stand for heaven. In the opposite corner, three broken lines stand for earth. The lines in the lower left corner represent fire, while the lines in the upper right represent water. The flag's white background symbolizes the purity of the Korean people and their peace-loving spirit.

The Taegeukgi is sometimes called the world's most philosophical flag. The yang and eum swirls and the sets of broken and unbroken lines are all symbols from Daoism (also spelled Taoism), an ancient Chinese philosophical system that was adopted by the Koreans.

The Taegeukgi was first proclaimed Korea's flag in 1883, during the Joseon dynasty. It became the flag of South Korea in 1950.

The National Government of South Korea

South Korea's national government has three branches—executive, legislative, and judicial. The president heads the executive branch and represents the country. South Korea's president is elected directly by the people and can serve only one five-year term. The president proposes laws to the legislature and carries out laws passed by the legislature. He or she also serves as commander-in-chief of the armed forces and has the power to declare war. In addition, the president appoints the prime minister, the chief justice of the supreme court, and members of the State Council.

The prime minister assists the president. The State Council is made up of the president, the prime minister, and the heads of

South Korea's Political Leaders

Roh Moo-hyun (1946–) served as South Korea's president from 2003 to 2008. He was born in Gimhae, a small farming village in southeastern South Korea. Roh taught himself law and passed the bar exam to become a lawyer. He worked as a human rights attorney, defending pro-democracy and labor-rights activists. In the 1980s and 1990s, Roh served brief terms in the National Assembly. As president, he worked to open the government to more people. He also worked to have economic growth that benefited all Koreans and to gain peace on the Korean Peninsula through better relations with North Korea.

From April 2006 to April 2007, Han Myeong-sook (1944–) served as South Korea's first female prime minister. Han was born in Pyongyang, North Korea, before her family moved south. She graduated from Ewha Woman's University with a degree in French literature. She also has degrees in theology and women's studies. From 1979 to 1981, she was imprisoned on charges of teaching pro-communist ideas to farmers, workers, and poor women. Since 2000, Han has been a member of the National Assembly. She has championed women's rights during her time in government.

In January 2007, Ban Ki-moon (1944–) became secretary-general of the United Nations. Ban was born in Eumseong, in central South Korea, and graduated in 1970 from Seoul University with a degree in international relations. In 1985, he received a master's degree from the John F. Kennedy School of Government at Harvard University. Ban has served in many positions in South Korea's Foreign Ministry. In 2003, he became President Roh's foreign-policy advisor, and he was named minister of foreign affairs and trade in 2004. Ban has said that as secretary-general, he will be actively involved in helping solve conflicts in Sudan, the Middle East, and North Korea.

NATIONAL GOVERNMENT OF SOUTH KOREA

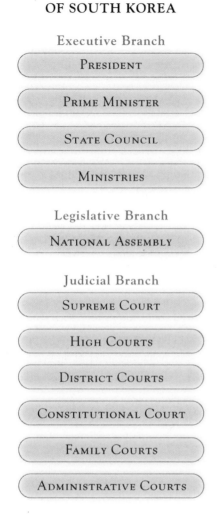

Executive Branch

President

Prime Minister

State Council

Ministries

Legislative Branch

National Assembly

Judicial Branch

Supreme Court

High Courts

District Courts

Constitutional Court

Family Courts

Administrative Courts

Above right: **South Korea's National Assembly is in session for about one hundred days each year.**

ministries. Each ministry handles a different part of South Korea's government. They include the ministry of agriculture and forestry, the ministry of justice, and the ministry of unification.

The National Assembly, South Korea's lawmaking body, has 273 members. They are elected to four-year terms and can be reelected. The National Assembly passes laws and approves the national budget. It also declares war and can make a motion to impeach, or remove, the president or other elected officers.

The supreme court is South Korea's top court. It hears appeals from high courts. The high courts in turn hear appeals of cases decided in district courts, family courts, and administrative courts. The constitutional court works to safeguard the constitution and protect people's rights. This court also holds impeachment trials upon a motion by the National Assembly.

The President's Home

The president of South Korea lives and works in the Blue House in Seoul. This building's name comes from its blue ceramic-tile roof. Surrounded by mountains, a stream, and a river, the location of the Blue House is considered to be lucky. The Blue House compound includes the main government office building, the presidential residence, a guesthouse, and a press hall. The buildings are modeled on traditional Korean architecture.

The National Anthem

South Korea's national anthem was first performed in 1896. At the time, it was often sung to the tune of "Auld Lang Syne." Korean music was written for it in 1937, and the song was adopted as the national anthem when South Korea was founded in 1948. Here is a translation of the lyrics.

Until the East Sea's waves are dry,
Baekdusan worn away,
God watch o'er our land forever!
Our country forever!

CHORUS:

Rose of Sharon, thousand miles of range and river land!
Guarded by her people, ever may Korea stand!

Like that Namsan armored pine,
standing on duty still, wind or frost,
unchanging ever, be our resolute will.

CHORUS

In autumn's arching evening sky,
crystal, and cloudless blue,
Be the radiant moon our spirit,
steadfast, single, and true.

CHORUS

With such a will, such a spirit,
loyalty, heart and hand,
Let us love, come grief, come gladness,
this, our beloved land!

CHORUS

Military Forces

South Korea maintains a large military. The South Korean government feels that it must do so to deter North Korea from acting aggressively or attacking. All South Korean men between twenty and thirty years of age must serve for twenty-four to twenty-eight months in the military.

South Korean men cannot leave the country for an extended period of time until they have performed this duty. An additional 4.5 million South Koreans are in the reserves.

Cadets march in formation at the Korea Military Academy.

Relations with North Korea

The two Koreas began moving closer together in 1970. In that year, the two countries recognized each other's government. In 1972, they began talks about reunification and about bringing together families that had been separated by the Korean War. Little came of the talks, however. In the 1990s, North Korea began reaching out again. In the late 1990s, some South Koreans visited family members in North Korea for the first time since 1950. North Korea also allowed small groups of South Korean tourists to enter the country. In 2000, the meeting in North Korea between the presidents of the two countries was a high point in Korean relations.

North Korean leader Kim Jong Il (left) and South Korean president Kim Dae-jung look at papers at the historic first meeting between the leaders of the two Koreas in 2000.

South Korea's main remaining problem with North Korea is North Korea's nuclear weapons programs. In 2003, North Korea announced that it was making nuclear weapons. Then, in October 2006, North Korea performed an underground nuclear test. Talks among South Korea, North Korea, Japan, China, Russia, and the United States have taken place off and on since 2003. In 2007, North Korea agreed to end its nuclear weapons program. The issue remains unsettled, however.

Seoul: Did You Know This?

Seoul is located on the Han River in northwestern South Korea. Founded in 1392 as the capital of the Joseon dynasty, Seoul is now the largest city on the Korean Peninsula, with a population of about 10,300,000. The city was devastated during the Korean War but rebuilt quickly. Today, it is a bustling city filled with cars and people.

Seoul is South Korea's commercial, cultural, and industrial center. Important industries include food processing and textile manufacture. Attractions include sections of the original city walls, five Joseon palaces, the National Museum, the National Folk Museum (above), the Jogyesa Temple, and the Jongmyo Shrine. Popular shopping spots include the Dongdaemun Market, the Namdaemun Market, and Itaewon Shopping Street.

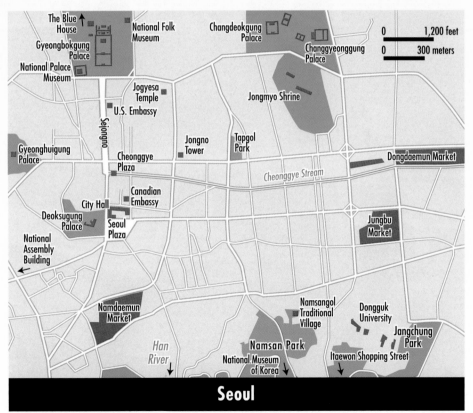

The Blue House
Gyeongbokgung Palace
National Palace Museum
National Folk Museum
Changdeokgung Palace
Changgyeonggung Palace
0 1,200 feet
0 300 meters
Jogyesa Temple
Sejongno
U.S. Embassy
Jongmyo Shrine
Gyeonghuigung Palace
Jongno Tower
Tapgol Park
Cheonggye Plaza
Cheonggye Stream
Dongdaemun Market
Canadian Embassy
City Hall
Deoksugung Palace
Seoul Plaza
Jungbu Market
National Assembly Building
Namdaemun Market
Namsangol Traditional Village
Dongguk University
Jangchung Park
Itaewon Shopping Street
Han River
Namsan Park
National Museum of Korea

Seoul

A Prosperous Economy

SOUTH KOREA'S ECONOMY HAS GROWN SO MUCH SINCE the 1960s that the country is known as the Miracle on the Han River. South Korea has a free-enterprise economy. Farmers own their land. Groups of people own and run companies, factories, banks, and a stock market. By 2007, South Korea had the world's eleventh-largest economy.

Opposite: **Rice is the leading crop in South Korea.**

A hardworking farmer tends her fields on Jeju Island.

Money Facts

The currency in South Korea is the *won*. Paper money comes in values of 1,000, 5,000, and 10,000 won. Coins have values of 10, 50, 100, and 500 won. In 2007, US$1 equaled 917 won.

The colorful bills show images of important people or places in Korean history. For example, the 5,000-won note shows Yi I, one of Korea's most prominent Confucian scholars.

South Korea's economy has occasionally faced rough times. In 1997, a financial crisis hit most countries in Asia, including South Korea. The value of South Korea's currency dropped and the stock market fell, causing the economy to

What South Korea Grows, Makes, and Mines	
Agriculture (2004)	
Rice	6,800,000 metric tons
Cabbage	2,800,000 metric tons
Watermelon	760,000 metric tons
Manufacturing (2001)	
Cement	52,046,000 metric tons
Steel	45,400,000 metric tons
Cars	3,150,000 units
Mining	
Coal (2004)	3,247,000 metric tons
Feldspar (2003)	477,000 metric tons
Iron ore (2003)	161,000 metric tons

collapse. Many businesses closed, fewer goods were produced, and thousands of people lost their jobs. South Korea's government quickly stepped in. It arranged for international loans and made changes in how business was conducted. By 2000, the country's economy was once again booming.

In some remote parts of South Korea, farmers still use oxen to plow fields.

Farming and Fishing

About 6 percent of South Korean workers are farmers. Their main crop is rice, but they also grow large amounts of vegetables such as cabbage, onions, and sweet potatoes. Fruit crops of melons, pears, persimmons, and peaches are also plentiful in South Korea. The Daegu area is known for its apples. The warm climate of Jeju Island produces pineapples and big tangerines. South Korea's farmers also raise beef and dairy cattle, hogs, and chickens.

South Korean markets sell many kinds of seafood, including octopus.

Fishing makes up a small but important part of the country's economy. Abalones, cod, king crabs, pollack, and squid are plentiful in South Korea's eastern waters. In the western waters are blue crabs, lobsters, shrimps, and surf clams. Fish and shellfish found in southern waters include anchovies, mackerel, mussels, and octopuses. Much of the catch is exported.

Women on Jeju Island are famous harvesters of the sea. They are known as free divers because they go underwater to great depths without breathing equipment. These women gather kelp, seaweed, and oysters.

Mining and Manufacturing

South Korea's most plentiful minerals are coal, feldspar, and iron ore. They are in small supply, however, and less than 1 percent of South Korea's workers are employed in mining. South Korea must import most mining products. Many of these imports, such as coal, gold, and zinc, come from North Korea. Oil and coal are South Korea's main cooking and heating fuels. Hydroelectric plants and four nuclear power plants provide much of South Korea's electric power.

Manufacturing employs about 26 percent of South Korea's workers. Cement and steel are important industries in the fast-growing nation. They are used to construct buildings and roads. In fact, the world's third-largest steelmaker is South Korea's Posco. More South Koreans work in industries making clothing, shoes, and textiles than in any other industry. Food processing is also a major industry in South Korea. The country is best known, however, as one of the world's biggest producers of cars, computers, computer parts, and other electronic equipment.

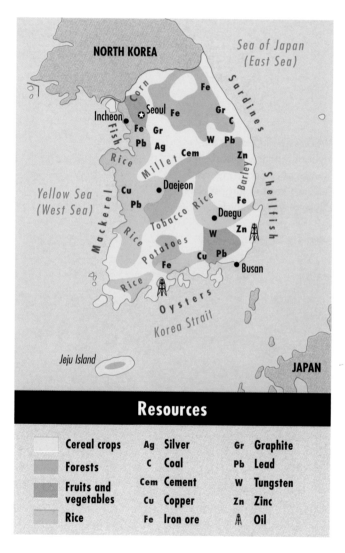

Resources

Cereal crops	Ag	Silver	Gr	Graphite
Forests	C	Coal	Pb	Lead
Fruits and vegetables	Cem	Cement	W	Tungsten
Rice	Cu	Copper	Zn	Zinc
	Fe	Iron ore	⚒	Oil

How Much Does It Cost?

	Price in Won	Price in U.S. Dollars
T-shirt	6,000-12,000	6.50–13.00
Bowl of noodles	3,500	3.78
Dinner in a nice restaurant	50,000	54.05
Apple	1,000	1.08
Ice cream cone	700–1,000	0.76–1.08
Liter (0.26 gallons) bottle of water	1,000	1.08
Liter (0.26 gallons) of gasoline	1,500	1.62
Movie ticket	7,000	7.57

Workers build cars at the Hyundai plant in Ulsan, southeast of Seoul. Hyundai is South Korea's largest producer of motor vehicles.

Most of these goods are made by about thirty huge companies. The leader is Samsung, the world's largest maker of memory chips. Samsung is also well known for its line of cell phones. Other well-known South Korean companies are Lucky-Goldstar (LG), Sunkyung (SK), and Hyundai. SK is South Korea's largest oil refinery, and LG is known for televisions, computer monitors, and cell phones. South Korea is the world's sixth-largest carmaker. Hyundai produces most of Korea's cars, trucks, buses, and merchant ships. Cars are also made by Daewoo and Kia. Hyundai and Kia have manufacturing plants in the United States and in other countries.

Tourists take pictures at a
historic gate in Seoul.

In 2003, Hyundai established an industrial park near
Gaeseong, North Korea. About nine hundred South Korean
manufacturing companies plan to build factories in the park.
By 2007, about forty South Korean factories had opened,
employing about fifteen thousand North Koreans making
goods such as clothes and shoes. Eventually, the industrial
park aims to provide 730,000 North Koreans with jobs.

Service Industries

About 67 percent of South Korea's workers are employed in
service industries. Tourism, trade, and transportation are the
country's most important service industries.

Tourism has been important to South Korea for many
years. In 2006, about six million people from other countries visited South Korea. They spent about US$5.2 billion
at hotels, restaurants, national parks, and museums. South
Koreans also travel about their own country, enjoying the

South Korea's new high-speed rail lines cut travel time between Seoul and Busan by one-third.

mountains, beaches, and parks. Some tourists in South Korea stay at inns called *yeogwan*. The inns have traditional heated *ondol* floors. Guests sleep on the floor on cotton mattresses.

Trade and Transportation

South Korea exports far more than it imports. The country's largest exports are electronics products, ships, cars, and chemicals. Crude oil is one of South Korea's largest imports. China, the United States, and the European Union are South Korea's main trading partners. Since 1998, trade between South Korea and North Korea has opened up. South Korea imports much-needed mining products from North Korea and exports rice to North Korea.

Railroads and highways connect major cities and towns in South Korea. In 2004, a high-speed rail line opened between Seoul and Busan. The trains can travel up to 185 miles (298 km) per hour. South Korea has more than 62,000 miles (100,000 km) of highways. About 10 million cars travel over these roads.

In 2000, work began to rebuild two stretches of railroad track that would link North Korea and South Korea. In May 2007, the first trains ran on these tracks. In the east, a train from North Korea traveled across the DMZ to Chejin in South Korea. In the west, a train left Munsan, South Korea, headed for Gaeseong, North Korea. Two highways also cross the DMZ. One ends at the industrial park near Gaeseong. The other crosses the eastern DMZ, carrying South Korean tourists into North Korea.

System of Weights and Measures

The metric system is the official system of weights and measures in South Korea, but traditional weights and measures are still used, too. For example, in South Korea 1 *guan* equals 8.27 pounds, which equals 3.75 kilograms. And 1 *pyeong* equals 36 square feet, which equals 3.3 square meters.

Historic sites such as Gyeongbokgung Palace attract millions of tourists to South Korea.

One People,
One Language

Although few people from other countries immigrate to South Korea, millions of Koreans now live throughout the world. Koreans have been immigrating to the United States since 1903. The first immigrants arrived in the Hawaiian Islands and worked on sugar and pineapple plantations. After the Korean War, many more Koreans left their war-torn land to make homes on the mainland of the United States. Today, more than one million people of Korean descent live in the United States. Most live in or near cities such as Los Angeles, New York, Chicago, and Seattle. Several thousand Koreans also live in Japan. Many of their families were forced to move there when Japan occupied the Korean Peninsula.

Korean signs dominate a Korean American neighborhood in Los Angeles, California. The United States is home to about 1.3 million people of Korean descent.

Creating an Alphabet

During the 1400s, King Sejong had his scholars create an alphabet for the Korean language. Until that time, Koreans used Chinese characters when writing. The Chinese written language has thousands of characters. Instead of putting together a few letters to form many words, the Chinese have a separate character for each word or idea. This makes learning written Chinese difficult. In Sejong's time, only scholars could read and write. Sejong wanted more of his people to have the pleasure of reading and writing.

Sejong's scholars developed the hangeul alphabet. At first, only women and common people used hangeul. Scholars continued to use Chinese characters. Only after World War II did hangeul become the official system for writing the Korean language. Now, each October 9, South Korea celebrates Hangeul Day in honor of the adoption of the alphabet in 1446.

The Korean Language

South Korea has one written and spoken language—the Korean language. When spoken, Korean is not closely related to either Chinese or Japanese, but it has adopted many words from those languages. Like Japanese, it is part of the proto-Altaic language group of central Asia. Turkish and classical Mongolian also belong to this language group. Although there is only one Korean language, there are several Korean dialects. Most Koreans can understand them without too much difficulty.

Written Korean looks quite different from English. Most European languages such as English are written in the letters of the Latin alphabet. The Korean language, however, uses the hangeul alphabet. It has ten vowels and fourteen consonants. The hangeul alphabet has no letters or sounds for *f*, *q*, *v*, *w*, *x*, and *z*. Hangeul is a phonetic alphabet—each letter has a distinct sound. The letters can be combined to form a large vocabulary of words. In South Korea, some two thousand Chinese characters are also used in writing, mainly in newspapers and academic books.

The Hangeul Alphabet

Hangeul Vowels	English Vowels	Hangeul Consonants	English Consonants
ㅏ	a	ㄱ	g, k
ㅑ	ya	ㄴ	n
ㅓ	eo	ㄷ	d, t
ㅕ	yeo	ㄹ	r, l
ㅗ	o	ㅁ	m
ㅛ	yo	ㅂ	b/p
ㅜ	u	ㅅ	s
ㅠ	yu	ㅇ	ng
ㅡ	eu	ㅈ	j
ㅣ	i	ㅊ	ch
		ㅋ	k
		ㅌ	t
		ㅍ	p
		ㅎ	h

A Korean family dressed in traditional clothing. The average Korean family has 1.3 children.

At one time, written Korean used accent marks and apostrophes to indicate pronunciation of some vowels. In 2000, the South Korean government dropped the accents and the apostrophes to make the language easier to write using computer keyboards.

Three Parts of Korean Names

Korean names usually have three parts. The family name comes first. The second part is a generation name, which is shared by all family members of the same sex in that generation. Last comes a given, or personal, name. Some South Koreans hyphenate their given name. They use a lowercase letter at the beginning of the given name, as in Chung Kyung-wha. Others use a capital letter at the beginning of each of their three names, such as Sun Myung Moon. Still others combine their generation and given names, such as Park Eunkyeong instead of Park Eun Kyeong.

A married woman does not take her husband's name. If a woman is called Mrs. Kim, that means she's married and that her father's family name is Kim. Women are usually called by their relationship to their husband or children. For example, if Mrs. Kim marries Mr. Park, she will known as "Mr. Park's wife." When Mrs. Kim becomes a mother, she will be known by the name of her oldest child, for example, "Eun-kyeong's mother."

Koreans rarely use given names when talking to one another. They usually use titles, such as Mrs., Director, or Principal, or they refer to one another by their station in the family, such as Elder Sister or Younger Brother.

Education

South Koreans place a high value on education. Students must attend school for at least nine years. A typical day for a middle school student begins at 8:20 in the morning and ends at about 4:00 in the afternoon. On Saturdays, the school day ends at noon. Students study subjects such as the Korean language, English, Chinese characters, math, natural science, biology, history, sociology, ethics, and physical education.

Most students go on to high school and then college. The entire country has one college admissions test. It is given just once a year. Students spend their last year in high school studying for this test. When they are preparing for the test, they do not go on vacations or take part in family celebrations or holidays. How well students do on this test determines which college or university they will attend. South Korea has more than 120 colleges and universities. Seoul National University, Korea University, and Yonsei University are the most prestigious. Graduating from one of those universities brings higher social status and better jobs.

Korea University was established in 1905. It has a strong reputation in business, law, and the social sciences.

Many Religions

SOUTH KOREANS FOLLOW MANY RELIGIONS AND BELIEF systems. These include Shamanism, Buddhism, Confucianism, Daoism, and Christianity. Many of these began elsewhere. Buddhism began in India and came to Korea through China. Confucianism and Daoism came directly from China. Christianity first came to Korea through China. Then, missionaries from Europe and the United States set up churches on the Korean Peninsula. Cheondogyo was created in Korea in reaction to Western learning and religions.

Opposite: **Gupodong Catholic Church in Anseong was built in 1922. The steeple was added in 1955.**

Long ago, Buddhist scriptures were engraved on woodblocks.

Religions of South Korea

Religion	Percentage
Buddhism	23%
Protestantism	20%
Roman Catholicism	7%
Confucianism	3%
Other (Shamanism, Islam, Cheondogyo)	1%
No religion	46%

Almost half of South Koreans say they follow some religion. Many of them accept the beliefs of more than one religion. For example, Christians might also offer prayers at a Buddhist shrine. Buddhists may take part in ancestor worship. Statistics about the country's religions always differ enormously. One reason for this is that many people have adopted the ideals of Confucianism but do not consider themselves active believers. The same applies to Shamanism. Not many people would call themselves active believers, but when large Shamanic village rituals take place, many people join in.

Ancient Natural Belief Systems

Shamanism is Korea's oldest religion. It has been practiced since ancient times. The center of Shamanism is the shaman, or *mudang*. As in the past, the mudang is usually a woman who acts as a link, a negotiator, between the living and the dead. The mudang contacts spirits through a ceremony called *kut*. During the ceremony, the mudang goes into a trance. It is believed that while in this trance, the mudang can see the future, cast out evil spirits, and ask for good fortune from kind

Music is central to Shamanist ceremonies.

spirits. A kut is sometimes held before a new business opens or to bring peace to a troubled family. Shamanism holds that all natural things have spirits or souls. This includes rocks, trees, streams, and mountains. Shaman spirit posts carved with scary faces—they look something like totem poles—still stand at

the entrance to some small villages. They were supposed to keep evil out of the villages. Today, between two million and three million South Koreans use the services of mudangs.

A mudang sings and dances as she goes into a trance.

Daoism is another belief that is based on nature. *Dao*, which means "the Way," is more a philosophy than a religion. The philosopher Laozi began this belief system in China in the 500s B.C. Daoism had reached Korea by the 100s B.C. Through Daoism, people are supposed to gain an understanding of nature's laws. It teaches that living in harmony with nature leads to prosperity and long life. Few Koreans practice Daoism today. Still, the Daoist *yang* and *eum* symbols of balance in the universe are seen throughout the country, most notably on South Korea's flag. The broken and unbroken black lines on the flag are also Daoist symbols.

The teachings of Confucius emphasized personal morality and the proper behavior of governments. His philosophy had great influence throughout East Asia.

Confucianism is not a religion like Buddhism or Christianity. There are no priests or monks, no god, no churches, and no worship rituals. Instead, Confucianism is a system of relationships with a code of behavior. When followed, this system ensures a well-ordered society. Confucius (551–479 B.C.) was a Chinese teacher and philosopher. He developed this code of conduct. According to Confucius, there are five ranks of superior/subordinate relationships: ruler/subject or government/citizen, father/son, older person/younger person, husband/wife, and friend/friend. In each relationship, the weaker or younger person submits to the stronger or older person. The stronger person is obliged to protect the weaker one. According to Confucianism, there is only equality in the relationship between friends, and then only if the two people are the same age and gender.

In Confucianism, respect for one's elders leads to respect for ancestors. Thus, Confucianism also calls for special ceremonies of ancestor worship. At one time, Confucianism required that government officials be scholars who had passed a rigorous civil service examination. To prepare for this test, young men spent years studying in Confucian academies.

Historians believe that Confucianism was introduced to Korea in the first centuries A.D. Later, it became the official philosophy or state religion of the Joseon dynasty. Koreans followed Confucianism so strictly that Chinese visitors said that Korea was more Confucian than China. Today, South Koreans still practice the ideas of Confucius. They show respect to their parents, honor their ancestors, maintain strong ties with all their relatives, show loyalty to their company or school, and have life-long friends. Through Confucianism, South Koreans have a strong sense of community. When something bad happens, such as the economic crisis in 1997, everyone in the country works together with the government to pull South Korea out of trouble. The Confucian attitude toward studying has carried over to regular schools and colleges. A small number of families still send their sons to after-school Confucian academies to become Confucian scholars.

South Korean students take part in the Seokjeonje celebration, which honors Confucius.

Today, South Korea has more than two hundred Confucian academies. Each academy has a library, a lecture hall, sleeping rooms, a shrine, and a pavilion. Twice a year, ceremonies are held at the academies to honor Confucius and Korean Confucian scholars. In the spring, South Korean government officials put on colorful Confucian ceremonial robes at the Jongmyo Shrine in Seoul to honor the Joseon kings. In September, the Seokjeonje ceremony honors Confucius's birthday at South Korea's main Confucian shrine.

Buddhism

Siddhartha Gautama founded Buddhism in India around 528 B.C. Later, he became known as the Buddha, "the Enlightened One." Enlightenment is the goal of all Buddhists. Enlightenment is achieved when a person eliminates all desire. Buddhists believe desire is the cause of all suffering. Until people attain enlightenment, they must go through a cycle of birth, death, and rebirth known as reincarnation. Besides the Buddha, there are many gods and goddesses in the Buddhist religion.

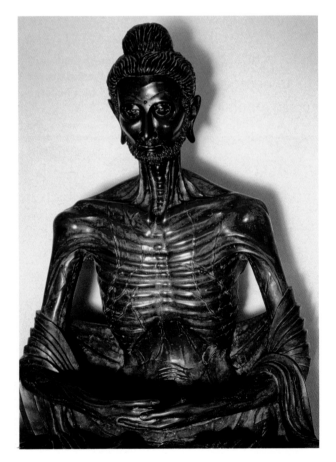

A bronze statue of Siddhartha Gautama. Siddhartha prayed and fasted before achieving enlightenment.

Buddhism entered Korea from China in the A.D. 300s. It became the state religion in each of the Three Kingdoms, as well as in Unified Silla and during the Goryeo dynasty. By the middle of the twentieth century, Buddhism was considered old-fashioned. The government encouraged its revival, however, and by the 1970s, the number of Buddhists had begun to increase. Many Buddhist temples were rebuilt. Today, South Korea is home to more than eleven thousand Buddhist temples and more than twenty-six thousand Buddhist monks and nuns. Buddhist temples can be found everywhere. Some lie off busy city streets. Others are in forested mountain hideaways.

Buddhist Treasures

Two of the most famous Buddhist temples in South Korea are Haeinsa (right) and Bulguksa (above). The Haeinsa Temple is the storage place for the *Tripitaka Koreana*, 81,340 wooden printing blocks that contain the world's most complete set of Buddhist teachings. More than fifty-two million Chinese characters are carved into the blocks.

Korean artisans took twenty-three years (751–774) to build the massive complex known as the Bulguksa Temple. *Bulguk* means "Land of the Buddha." The temple complex is located in the foothills near the ancient city of Gyeongju. It represents the height of Korea's Buddhist culture and art. In the courtyard stand two of Korea's most beautiful stone pagodas. The simplicity of the Seokgatap Pagoda symbolizes the spiritual way to enlightenment. The more decorative Dabotap Pagoda represents the desires of the world. Bulguksa is also noted for its two large, seated, bronze statues of the Buddha.

Worshippers fill the pews at the Yeoeuido Full Gospel Church in Seoul. The church seats about twelve thousand people.

Christianity

Christianity also first reached Korea through China. This religion teaches that Jesus Christ is the son of God and that he died to redeem the sins of all people. During the 1600s, officials of the Joseon dynasty carried Catholic writings into Korea. In 1784, the first Roman Catholic priests arrived in Korea. The government did not approve of Catholicism because Catholics were not allowed to take part in ancestor worship. In the early 1800s, thousands of Korean Catholics were executed.

In the late 1800s, after Korea had opened to trade with other countries, Protestant missionaries from England and the United States arrived. Both Catholic and Protestant missionaries established schools, universities, hospitals, and orphanages. During the Japanese occupation, Christian missionaries worked with Koreans to win back Korea's independence. In the past few decades, South Korean Christians have been outspoken supporters of democracy and human rights in their country.

Today, Christians are the second-largest religious group in Korea. They include Catholics and Protestant denominations such as Methodists, Presbyterians, and Anglicans. Many Koreans also belong to evangelical churches or the Church of Jesus Christ of Latter-day Saints (the Mormon church). South Korea has about 4.2 million Catholics and about 9.8 million Protestants.

The Yeoeuido Full Gospel Church in Seoul is one of the world's largest churches, with more than seven hundred

Catholics make up about 7 percent of the South Korean population. Their numbers have doubled in the last decade.

Korean Saints

Pope John Paul II visited Seoul in 1984 to celebrate the two hundredth anniversary of Catholicism coming to Korea. During his visit, he acknowledged the many Koreans who had died for their faith during the persecutions of the 1800s. He proclaimed 103 of them saints. This gave Korea the world's fourth-largest number of Catholic saints.

thousand members. South Korea's most prominent Catholic church is the Myeongdong Cathedral in Seoul. The Gothic-style building was completed in 1898 on the site of Korea's first Catholic church, which was built in 1784.

South Korean Catholics attend services at Myeongdong Cathedral.

Other Religions

In the 1860s, Choe Je-u began the Donghak Movement, or Eastern Learning Movement. This was a reaction to the Western learning that was being spread through Korea by the Catholic Church. The government executed Choe in 1863, but his movement gained many followers. They changed the movement's name to Cheondogyo, "Teachings of the Heavenly Way." The main beliefs of Cheondogyo are that all people are equal and that there is divinity, or God, in each person. Today, about one million South Koreans are followers of Cheondogyo.

In 1954, the Reverend Sun Myung Moon founded the Holy Spirit Association for the Unification of World Christianity, better known as the Unification Church. Its followers are called Moonies by its detractors. This church teaches that there is one God but not that Jesus Christ was divine. Followers believe that a savior, born in Korea, will marry the perfect woman and that the two of them will be the perfect parents of all mankind. Some of Moon's followers believe that he and his wife are these parents.

Moon has been convicted of tax evasion in the United States, and he and his church have been accused of fraud in some of the church's business ventures. Moon's Unification Church is perhaps best known for huge wedding ceremonies in which he marries hundreds of couples at one time.

The Unification Church often holds mass weddings. More than 4,600 couples were married at one time in a ceremony in Cheonan in 2005.

Arts: Old and New

98

SOUTH KOREA'S ARTS ARE A MIX OF THE TRADITIONAL AND the modern. South Koreans treasure their rich cultural heritage. At the same time, many South Korean musicians, artists, and actors are pushing Korean culture in new directions.

Opposite: **A woman prepares to play a traditional Korean hourglass drum.**

Traditional Crafts

Throughout the centuries, Korean artists and craftspeople have worked with paper, wood, cloth, and ceramics to create beautiful objects for everyday use. Geometric patterns of blue-green, red, and brown decorate much Korean craftwork. Symbols from nature, such as the sun and moon, cranes, fish, butterflies, trees, and streams are also common.

A tree graces the cover of a green ceramic jar.

Celadon, Korea's most famous pottery, was developed more than a thousand years ago. It uses bluish-green glazes and often includes inlaid designs of objects such as clouds and cranes. Celadon cups, bowls, pitchers, and vases are found in museums around the world. South Korean potters continue to make celadon and use traditional techniques and designs. In fact,

Bright bolts of silk cloth line the walls of a market in Seoul.

traditional kilns have been built so modern potters can re-create high-quality pottery today.

South Korean crafters also show their creativity with silk, hemp, ramie, and cotton cloth. *Bojagi* are colorful square wrapping cloths. Small pieces of leftover material are sewn together in geometric patchwork designs to make the bojagi squares. Long ago, Koreans believed that keeping things wrapped up brought good fortune. These square cloths come in various sizes and can be folded for use as money belts, backpacks, tablecloths, or laundry sacks. Some bojagi look like an envelope or pouch and have ties attached. Special bojagi used for weddings and other ceremonies are embroidered with designs of flowers and birds. Korean embroidery is called *jasu*. Besides decorating bojagi, jasu is found on traditional clothing, pillowcases, eyeglass cases, and purses. At one time, only nobles and royalty could wear or own clothing or cloth with jasu.

Korea is also famous for its paper crafts. In rural areas, mulberry-bark paper is still used for windows and interior sliding doors. Decorative jars, bowls, baskets, trays, stationery cases, and jewelry boxes are a few items that crafters still make from paper. They paste many layers of paper together to make the items strong. Colorful designs are painted on the paper, which is then varnished with a mixture of persimmon juice, rice glue, and oil. The most popular paper goods made today are lanterns displayed on the Buddha's birthday, fans, and kites.

Colorful paper lanterns hang from trees during a festival celebrating the Buddha's birthday.

Art

Early Korean art was divided into paintings for the noble class and folk paintings. Paintings for the noble class focused on flowers, birds, and landscapes with trees, water, and stones. Artists used restrained brushwork and neutral colors. Rarely were people shown in these paintings. Folk paintings also used objects from nature but presented them with humor. Brushwork in folk paintings was lively, and the artists used bright colors. The tiger was a favorite object in Korean folk paintings. The animals were often shown as friendly, funny, or even stupid.

Early Korean artists also did paintings with religious themes. They showed Buddhist gods or people observing the

Artist of the People

Kim Hong-do (1745–1806) was an artist during the Joseon dynasty. Kim painted portraits of royalty and landscapes of real scenes from throughout the country. He is best remembered for his scenes of everyday people at work and at play. He painted schoolrooms (right), *ssireum* wrestlers, and village musicians and dancers. These paintings left a record of the lives of common people.

Paik Nam-june was known for using televisions in his work. This piece, called *Turtle*, includes more than a hundred TV screens.

Confucian ideas of loyalty and respect. Buddhist deities were the subject of many early Korean sculptures. At the Seokguram Grotto, thirty-nine figures of Buddhist gods are chiseled in the wall. They surround a tall statue of the Buddha.

Many modern South Korean artists use the spirit of traditional art in their works. For example, Sanjong uses black ink in a controlled stroke, but his paintings express a modern sense of freedom. One of Korea's most popular modern artists is the sculptor Paik Nam-june. His sculptures include television sets, speakers, and musical instruments. They encourage people to examine what they really see and hear on television. Paik's well-known pieces include *V-ramid*, a pyramid with masks and television screens, and *Man on Horseback*, a figure made from television sets.

The gayageum makes soft, delicate sounds. It can be played either by plucking or vibrating the strings.

Traditional Music and Dance

The most famous traditional Korean song genre is *pansori*. These long, dramatic songs are performed by a person who is accompanied by a performer playing a *buk* (barrel drum).

Traditional singers are frequently accompanied by a *gayageum*, a twelve-string zither. Other traditional stringed instruments include the *ajaeng*, a seven-string zither, and the *haegeum*, a two-string fiddle. Besides the *buk*, other Korean percussion instruments include the *kkwaenggwari* (small gong), the *jing* (large gong), and the *janggo* (hourglass drum). Drums and gongs are played by dancers in many folk dances, as well as by drum and gong ensembles. Korean wind instruments are played in small groups with other instruments. The main wind instruments are the *daegeum* (large bamboo flute), the *hojeok* (conical oboe), the *piri* (bamboo oboe), and the *tungso* (vertical bamboo flute).

Traditional Korean dances include folk, court, and religious performances. *Pulgmul nori* is a popular farmers' dance. The dancers' hats have long streamers. The dancers swirl the streamers in wide loops. In some folk dances, the performers wear large, full-head masks. In the past, the dancers wore masks to hide their identity because they were making fun of the ruling class. Today, the dances are performed as entertainment. *Taepyeongmu* ("Dance of Great Peace") is a court dance from the Joseon dynasty. It is performed as a prayer for national peace and prosperity. In *Seungmu*, a Buddhist dance, the dancers move in harmony with their surroundings, which creates a dreamlike effect.

Folk dancers perform at a festival in Suwon.

South Koreans also like Western music. Several South Koreans have gained worldwide fame for their work in Western classical music. Yun Isang wrote more than 150 works, including symphonies and operas with political themes. An Ik-tae wrote South Korea's national anthem as well as *Korea Fantasia*, a long piece that expresses Korea's highs and lows during its five-thousand-year history. Jo Su-mi is Korea's most famous opera star. She has sung in opera houses around the world.

Rain is one of the biggest pop stars in South Korea. He is also a successful actor.

Popular music is part of the "Korean Wave" of culture that has quickly spread to other Asian countries and around the world. Rain (Jeong Ji-hun) and BoA (Gweon Bo-a) are two of South Korea's most popular stars. Rain sings pop, hip-hop, and rhythm and blues and incorporates taekwondo moves into his dance steps. Early in 2006, he performed at Madison Square Garden in New York City. Later that year, *Time* magazine named him one of the "100 Most Influential People Who Shape Our World." BoA sings pop songs in Korean, Japanese, and Chinese and plays the piano. In 2004, MTV Asia named her the Most Influential Artist in Asia.

Koreans have been making films since 1919, with the production of the drama *Righteous Revenge*. The South Korea film industry really took off after 1990. The 1993 film *Seopyeonje* ("The Western Style") told the story of a family of pansori singers and the problems they had in the modern world. The 1999 spy thriller *Siri* was a box-office smash. The films of writer and director Kim Ki-duk are popular in Europe and the United States.

Jeon Do-yeon is one of the most respected actresses in South Korea.

His best-known film is *Spring, Summer, Fall, Winter . . . and Spring*, which follows the lives of Buddhist monks through five seasons. Bong Jun-ho makes horror and murder mysteries with a sly sense of humor. In 2007, his film *The Host*, about a monster lizard, received good reviews in the United States.

In 2000, *Chunhyangjeon*, the story of a young woman's loyalty to her husband, was the first South Korean film to be entered at Cannes, the world's most famous film festival. In 2007, Jeon Do-yeon won the best actress award at Cannes for her role as a young widow in *Secret Sunshine*. South Korea now has its own film festivals each year in Busan, Bucheon, and Jeonju.

South Korean television dramas are eagerly watched in Taiwan, Thailand, Malaysia, China, Japan, and Vietnam. Popular shows have included *A Jewel in the Palace* and *Winter Sonata*. The latter series turned actor Bae Yong-jun into one of Japan's biggest heartthrobs ever.

The Jikji printing plates seen here are the oldest evidence of movable metal type printing in the world. The plates were used to print books in Cheongju, Korea, in 1377.

Korea's early literature was written using Chinese characters. Histories were among the first works produced. During the Goryeo dynasty, two accounts of the Three Kingdoms period were written. The most important history of the Joseon dynasty is the *Joseon Wangjo Sillok*. This history also includes an encyclopedia with sections on agriculture, the economy, music, geography, and many other subjects.

Korea has many traditional forms of poetry. The longest-lasting style is called *sijo*. This form of poetry has three lines with about fifteen syllables per line. Sijo are personal poems about feelings such as love, grief, or anger. Some sijo, however, have political or satirical themes. Throughout history, women have been more likely to write love sijo, while men have written political sijo.

After the hangeul alphabet was invented, some Korean writers began using it instead of Chinese characters. Heo Kyun (1569–1618) wrote the first novel in hangeul, *The Story of Hong Kiltong*. It concerns a man who sets up a classless society on an island without nobles and their laws. Noblewomen in the Korean court also wrote novels using hangeul. The most famous of these is *The Memoirs of Lady Hyegyeong*, which was written by Princess Hyegyeong (1735–1815). She based it on the true story of how her father-in-law, the king, killed her husband, his own son.

In recent decades, South Korean writers have been influenced by Western ideas. The poet Kim Soweol used ordinary speech and slang in his poems. Seo Cheongju's anthology *Unforgettable Things* has poems that describe the many changes in Koreans' lives since the 1950s. One of Korea's best-known novelists is Ahn Cheong-hyo. He writes his novels both in English and Korean.

Sports

The most famous sport to begin in Korea is *taekwondo*. South Koreans trace this martial art to the beginning of Korean civilization, but many argue that its current form is based on

Taekwondo became an official Olympic sport in 2000. South Korea's Myeong Seob-song (in red) won a bronze medal at the 2004 Olympics.

karate. At one time, taekwondo was part of Korea's national defense system. Before becoming a soldier, Korean men had to be skilled in taekwondo. Today, it is still used to discipline the mind, body, and spirit. People all over the world now practice taekwondo, and it is now an official Olympic sport.

The origins of *ssireum*, or Korean wrestling, can be traced back to about 37 B.C. Ssireum started as a competition among villagers and then became a martial art. Today, ssireum matches are held in stadiums and shown on TV. In ssireum, two wrestlers

South Korea in the Olympics

In 1988, the Summer Olympic Games were held in Seoul. For these games, South Korea built the Seoul Sports Complex, which includes the Olympic Stadium, two gymnasiums, an indoor swimming pool, and a baseball stadium. Other sports facilities and training areas were built in other parts of Seoul, as well as in Busan, where some events were played. More than 13,000 athletes from 160 countries took part in the games, although North Korea did not send a team. South Korea's athletes placed fourth in the overall medal count.

Koreans have long taken part in the Olympics. In the 1936 Olympics, Son Ki-jeong won gold in the marathon. He was part of Japan's team because at the time Japan ruled Korea. Hwang Yeong-jo won the gold medal in the marathon in 1992. In recent years, South Koreans have excelled at speed skating. In 2006, South Korean speed skaters came home with six gold, three silver, and two bronze medals.

Since 1948, South Korea and North Korea have sent separate teams to the Olympic Games. In the 2000 Summer Games in Sydney, Australia, the two teams marched together for the first time in the opening ceremonies.

wearing cloth sashes enter a ring filled with sand. They grab each other's sash, and each tries to push the other out of the ring.

Archery is another traditional Korean sport. Many South Korean women have become skilled at this sport, and some have won gold medals at the Olympics.

Soccer is enormously popular in South Korea. Children play soccer in their neighborhoods and at school. The South Korean men's national team has a huge following. Their fans are called Red Devils because they wear red shirts and caps. When South Korea made it to the semifinals during the 2002 World Cup, the world's biggest soccer competition, the streets of Seoul were filled with people in red. South Korea also has a women's national team.

In June 2002, hundreds of thousands of South Korean soccer fans poured into downtown Seoul to celebrate South Korea's victory over Spain in a World Cup match. Most of the fans wore red, the team color.

Jeonju World Cup Stadium

The Jeonju World Cup Stadium was built for the 2002 World Cup soccer tournament. The roof was designed to look like a traditional Korean folding fan. The columns and cables that hold up the roof look like the twelve-string gayageum, a traditional musical instrument.

The 2002 World Cup games were played in both South Korea and Japan. This was the first time that two countries hosted the World Cup. The South Korean team surprised the world and placed fourth—their best showing ever.

Professional baseball and golf have huge followings in South Korea. Several professional Korean baseball players have had international success. Park Chan-ho and Kim Byung-hyun have been pitchers on Major League teams in the United States, and Choi Hee-sup is a promising first baseman. In the world of golf, Choi Kyung-ju won three major men's world titles in 2002 and 2003. Pak Se-ri won four major women's championships in 1998 and was chosen Ladies' Rookie of the Year. At age twenty, she was the youngest woman to receive that honor. In 2007, she was inducted into the World Golf Hall of Fame. Pak's success has inspired many other young Korean women to become professional golfers, including Park Grace, Kim Mi-hyun, and Han Hee-won.

In recent years, more South Koreans have been taking part in sports. Tennis, bicycling, jogging, swimming, and hiking are a few of the more popular sports. In 1977, Ko Sang-don successfully climbed to the top of Mount Everest in Tibet. Since then, more South Koreans have become interested in climbing their country's many mountains.

Hikers make their way up the rocky slopes of Hallasan. Hiking and mountain climbing are growing in popularity in South Korea.

Everyday Life

SOUTH KOREAN MEN AND WOMEN WORK LONG HOURS ON farms and in factories, offices, and the home. South Korean children study hard in school and after school. They also find time to get together with family and friends.

Opposite: **Seoul is a big, bustling city.**

Family Life

The family holds a special place in the life of Koreans. Three of the five Confucian relationships deal with respect within the family: children for parents, wives for husbands, and juniors for elders. Parents and grandparents treasure their children.

The COEX Mall is the largest shopping center in South Korea. It includes about 260 stores.

Children treat their parents and grandparents with respect and take care of them in their old age. Younger brothers and sisters also respect their older brothers and sisters.

Korean Weddings

In the past, a Korean wedding began at the bride's home and ended with the groom taking his bride to his parent's home. During the ceremonies, the couple wore special wedding *hanbok*, traditional Korean clothing. Today, weddings take place in churches or in huge wedding halls. A South Korean bride usually wears a white, Western-style wedding gown, and the groom wears a dark suit. After the ceremony, the couple then change into *hanbok* and go to the groom's parents' home. There, they honor their parents with low bows and take part in a special tea ceremony. The bride's parents are expected to provide them with three keys: to a car, an apartment, and an office if the groom is a lawyer or doctor.

About 18 percent of South Koreans are under fifteen years of age.

In the past, a Korean household was made up of three generations. This included grandparents, parents, children, and even aunts and uncles. Today, most South Korean households have only two generations: parents and their children. In densely populated South Korea, most couples limit themselves to one or two children. Although couples still hope to have at least one son, families that have only daughters are becoming more acceptable. In South Korea, daughters now share equally in inheritance rights with sons. For hundreds of years, sons, and sometimes only the eldest son, could inherit family property.

Few South Korean mothers work outside the home. Mothers are called the "inside person" because their job is to raise their children and take care of the household. South Korean mothers spend many hours helping their children with schoolwork and taking them to after-school classes in English and math. South Korean fathers usually leave early in the morning for work. They are called the "outside person." Many evenings, they return home after the family has had dinner. Many South Korean men are unhappy because they face considerable pressure to succeed in society.

Hikers take in the view from a peak near Seoul.

South Korean families try to make the most of their time together. They go on bike rides and hike through parks, and they fish and play in nearby rivers and streams. They also keep in close contact with other family members, such as grandparents and aunts and uncles. Important family occasions include weddings, birthdays, and New Year's festivals.

Three Important Birthdays

Koreans use a method different from North Americans to count a person's age. When a baby is born, Koreans say he or she is in the first year, or "one." On Lunar New Year's Day, all Koreans gain a year, so the child is in his or her second year, or "two." Modern South Korean families also celebrate birthdays on the actual birth date with parties, gifts, and their own version of the song "Happy Birthday."

In the past, many South Korean children died in infancy. A ceremony called *baegil* was held for those who lived one hundred days. It was believed that they were then healthy enough to reach adulthood. At baegil, the baby was given its name. Baegil is still performed today. Family and friends offer thanks to the grandmother spirit who is believed to watch over infants. Everyone then enjoys a feast.

A child dressed in hanbok celebrates his first birthday.

On the first anniversary of a child's birth, Koreans hold a birthday celebration called *dol.* The child is dressed in traditional clothing called hanbok and then placed behind a low table filled with tall stacks of fruits, rice cakes, and other items. Whichever item the child picks up first is supposed to predict his or her future. Money means a career in business, while a piece of cake might lead to government service. A length of string points to a long life. A pencil means the child may become a scholar, and a musical instrument predicts a future musician.

A Korean's sixtieth birthday, called *hwangap,* has long been important for two reasons. In the past, not many people lived to be sixty years old. Also, the calendar used by Koreans is based on a sixty-year cycle. Each year of the sixty-year cycle has a different name. By living through the entire cycle, a person returns to the year of his or her birth. At hwangap, family and friends honor the sixty-year-old with deep bows and gifts. Today, many sixty-year-old Koreans observe their hwangap by taking a vacation.

Korean Meals

Korean foods are known for their variety, strong flavors, and hot spices. Slightly sticky white rice balances these flavors at every meal. In South Korea, people eat three meals a day. Rice and spicy pickled vegetables called *gimchi* are part of every

Shoppers can choose from a huge array of foods at this market in Busan.

South Korea's National Dish

Gimchi is South Korea's national dish. The first written description of making gimchi dates to about A.D. 1250. In South Korea, gimchi is served every day at every meal.

Basically, gimchi is pickled vegetables seasoned with red peppers. Vegetables used include Chinese cabbage, cucumbers, or radish roots. Onions, carrots, seaweed, garlic, and pine nuts are other ingredients in gimchi. There are about 170 varieties of gimchi. Two or three kinds of gimchi are served with each meal. Gimchi is also used as a fiery seasoning in soups and stews.

In the past, families made large crocks of gimchi, which they stored outdoors during the winter. Today,

some families still make their own gimchi. Large crocks of it can be seen on back porches throughout South Korean cities. Gimchi is also available in supermarkets. Since Gimchi also has many vitamins, Koreans believe it keeps them healthy. Gimchi is so important to South Koreans that there is even a Gimchi Museum in Seoul.

meal. A typical breakfast consists of soup, vegetables, meat or fish, rice, and gimchi. Lunch might be a salad, corn, meat, rice, and gimchi. Dinner may include beef and crab, beans, other vegetables, rice, and gimchi. Cold drinks such as fruit juices or punch are served before meals. Tea and a dessert of fruit or sweet rice cakes are served after dinner.

Korean meals are served on a low table with everyone sitting on the floor. Each person has his or her own bowls of rice and soup. Several bowls with side dishes of vegetables, meat, and fish are arranged in the center of the table, along with bowls of gimchi and soy-based sauces or pastes. Everyone takes the side dishes from these bowls with their chopsticks. They then might dip the food into a bowl of soy sauce or pick up some gimchi for seasoning.

Bulgogi

Like gimchi, *bulgogi* is closely linked to Korea. Unlike gimchi, bulgogi is not served every day. Instead, it is served on special occasions. *Bulgogi* means "fired meat" or "barbecue." Like most barbecue food, bulgogi is easy to make.

Ingredients

1 pound beef sirloin

$\frac{1}{4}$ cup soy sauce

1 teaspoon honey

1 tablespoon sugar

2 cloves garlic, minced

$\frac{1}{4}$ onion, chopped

2 teaspoons sesame oil

$\frac{1}{8}$ teaspoon ground black pepper

Leaf lettuce

Slices of green pepper

Directions

Have an adult help you with this recipe. First, cut the beef across the grain into thin slices. Tenderize each slice by tapping on it with the dull side of a knife. Mix the next seven ingredients in a bowl. Place the meat in the mixture. Cover the bowl and set it in the refrigerator for an hour.

Preheat the broiler of the oven or have someone fire up a barbecue grill for you. Then cook the meat slices on high heat for about 2 minutes on each side. Wrap the cooked meat with green pepper slices in lettuce leaves and serve.

Housing

Until the 1950s, almost all Koreans lived in houses. The houses were made with wood beams, clay walls, and thatch roofs. Only the homes of the wealthy had tile roofs. Rooms were separated by sliding doors made of mulberry paper. The most remarkable part of traditional housing was the heating system, called *ondol.* Channels under the floor carried hot air from the kitchen fire to other rooms in the house. Because the floors were warm, people sat on them to eat. At night, they pulled out mats to sleep on the floor.

Today, single-family homes are made of concrete and have tile roofs. These homes are mainly in suburbs and rural villages. Most South Koreans now live in large apartment buildings. The ondol heating system is still in use. In houses, pipes under the floors carry heated water. In apartment buildings, electric coils under the floors provide heat. In the summer, air conditioning is also provided through the ondol system. Most South Koreans still sleep on the floor and sit on the floor to eat, but some homes now have Western-style beds and tables and chairs.

More than 80 percent of South Koreans live in urban areas. Most urban South Koreans live in apartment buildings.

Hanbok

South Koreans almost always wear Western-style clothing. Traditional clothing called hanbok is worn, however, on holidays and special occasions. Parts of this costume date back to the A.D. 600s.

The woman's hanbok has a long, full, wrap-around skirt (*chima*) and a short jacket or blouse (*jeogori*) tied with a bow to one side. The man's hanbok has a short jacket (also called *jeogori*) and baggy pants (*baji*) that tie at the ankles. Men and women wear a long, full coat (*durumagi*) over their outfits. Hanbok often come in vivid colors. Both men and women wear colorful shoes with turned up toes as part of the hanbok. Because the hanbok has no pockets, men and women carry drawstring purses (*jumeoni*). Hanbok are also made for boys, girls, and infants. Because the hanbok is graceful and comfortable, some Korean fashion designers are making modern styles of hanbok, which some Koreans wear regularly.

Korean See-Saw

Nolddwigi was once a common game on Seollal. It was played by girls in hanbok. To play nolddwigi, a wide board is centered over a rolled up straw mat. One person sits on the middle of the board. Two girls stand on either end of the board. The first girl jumps up and lands on her end of the board, which sends the other girl into the air. When the second girl lands, the first girl is again sent up.

Holidays and Festivals in South Korea

Between national holidays and traditional festivals, Koreans have something to celebrate every month. Each province or city has its own festivals. For example, Jeju Island Province holds the World Festival for Island Cultures. The city of Jinhae celebrates the Cherry Blossom Festival in early spring, while the city of Geumsan holds the Ginseng Festival in September.

The two most important holidays in South Korea are Seollal and Chuseok. Seollal, the Lunar New Year, is the first

South Korea's National Holidays

New Year's Day	January 1
Seollal (Lunar New Year)	January or February
Independence Movement Day	March 1
Arbor Day	April 5
Children's Day	May 5
Memorial Day	June 6
Constitution Day	July 17
Liberation Day	August 15
Chuseok	September or October
National Foundation Day	October 3
Hangeul/National Alphabet Day	October 9
Christmas	December 25

big celebration of the year. It lasts for several days at the end of January or beginning of February. During Seollal, Koreans return to their hometowns or to their oldest relative's home. On the first day of Seollal, many people wear hanbok. The first thing in the morning, Korean families offer their deceased ancestors special foods in a ceremony called *charye*. Later, young members of the family perform *sebae*, a special low bow to their parents, grandparents, and other elders. The bow expresses wishes for happiness and good health in the coming year. In return, the elders give the children pouches of money called *sebae-don*. Then, they eat *tteokguk*, a soup with sliced rice cakes, meat, and vegetables. With this soup, Koreans acknowledge that they are one year older. Koreans add one year to their age on Seollal rather than on their calendar birthday.

After eating, people may play a traditional game. Boys spin tops in a game called *paengi-chigi*. Kite flying is also popular. Koreans say the kite takes away bad luck and brings good luck for the new year. These traditional games are becoming less common. Instead, many Koreans watch television or play video and computer games after eating.

During the nation's other major holiday, Chuseok, South Koreans give thanks for the good harvest in the fall. During the holiday, Korean families eat *songpyeon*, crescent-shaped rice cakes filled with sesame seeds, chestnut paste, or beans. In the morning, they visit their ancestors' graves. At the graves, they perform low bows, make offerings of the songpyeon, and clean the area around the grave.

South Koreans also celebrate patriotic holidays. Constitution Day marks the day that South Korea's constitution went into effect in 1948. On Liberation Day, South Koreans celebrate the end of Japanese rule over Korea with parades, fireworks, and speeches. This holiday is also celebrated in North Korea. In 2005, the two Koreas celebrated Liberation Day together for the first time during the Grand National Festival in Seoul.

Dancers perform at an event marking Korean liberation from Japanese colonial rule.

South Korea's people continue to honor important events in the past and to practice their traditional values and arts. They do not live in the past, however. They have forged ahead and built a modern, democratic, dynamic country. Today, South Korea is a global economic leader and a cultural force that echoes around the world.

Timeline

South Korean History

People are living on the Korean Peninsula.   **ca. 28,000** B.C.

The ancestors of Koreans move to the Korean Peninsula from central Asia.   **ca. 3000** B.C.

According to legend, Dangun founds Ancient Joseon.   **2333** B.C.

China conquers the northern part of the Korean Peninsula.   **108** B.C.

The kingdoms of Goguryeo, Silla, and Baekje are formed.   **ca. 57** B.C.

The Goguryeo Kingdom adopts Buddhism; a Confucian school is founded in Goguryeo.   **A.D. 300s**

Much of the Korean Peninsula is unified under the Silla Kingdom.   **668**

Wang Kon, founder of the Goryeo dynasty, unites the peninsula.   **935**

The Mongols invade the Korean Peninsula.   **1231**

Yi Song-gye, founder of the Joseon dynasty, takes power on the Korean Peninsula.   **1392**

The hangeul alphabet is invented.   **1446**

The Manchus invade Korea.   **1600s**

World History

2500 B.C.   Egyptians build the pyramids and the Sphinx in Giza.

563 B.C.   The Buddha is born in India.

A.D. **313**   The Roman emperor Constantine legalizes Christianity.

610   The Prophet Muhammad begins preaching a new religion called Islam.

1054   The Eastern (Orthodox) and Western (Roman Catholic) Churches break apart.

1095   The Crusades begin.

1215   King John seals the Magna Carta.

1300s   The Renaissance begins in Italy.

1347   The plague sweeps through Europe.

1453   Ottoman Turks capture Constantinople, conquering the Byzantine Empire.

1492   Columbus arrives in North America.

1500s   Reformers break away from the Catholic Church, and Protestantism is born.

1776   The U.S. Declaration of Independence is signed.

South Korean History

Japan forces Korea open to trade.	1876
Japan annexes Korea as a colony.	1910
Koreans stage major protests for independence.	1919
Korea is divided at the end of World War II.	1945
The Republic of Korea is established in South Korea.	1948
North Korea invades South Korea.	1950
The Korean War ends in a cease-fire.	1953
South Korea experiences a booming economy.	late 1970s
South Korea holds its first free and democratic elections.	1987
The Summer Olympic Games are held in Seoul.	1988
South Korea open diplomatic relations with China.	1992
Leaders of North Korea and South Korea meet for the first time; South Korean president Kim Dae-jung is awarded the Nobel Peace Prize.	2000
President Roh Moo-hyun is impeached and then reinstated.	2004
Ban Ki-moon of South Korea becomes secretary-general of the United Nations; leaders of North Korea and South Korea meet a second time.	2007

World History

1789	The French Revolution begins.
1865	The American Civil War ends.
1879	The first practical light bulb is invented.
1914	World War I begins.
1917	The Bolshevik Revolution brings communism to Russia.
1929	A worldwide economic depression begins.
1939	World War II begins.
1945	World War II ends.
1957	The Vietnam War begins.
1969	Humans land on the Moon.
1975	The Vietnam War ends.
1989	The Berlin Wall is torn down as communism crumbles in Eastern Europe.
1991	The Soviet Union breaks into separate states.
2001	Terrorists attack the World Trade Center in New York City and the Pentagon in Washington, D.C.

Fast Facts

Official name: Republic of Korea

Capital: Seoul

Official language: Korean

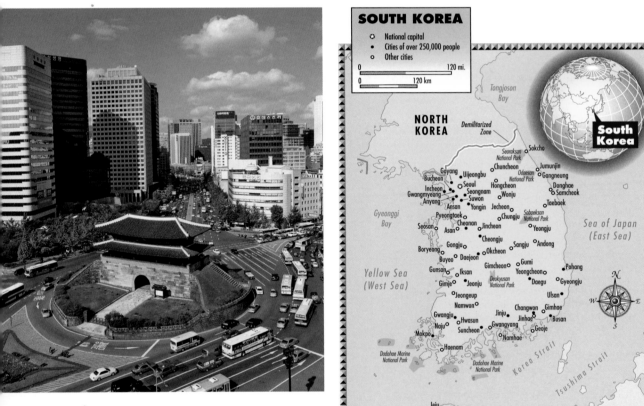

Seoul

South Korea's flag

Demilitarized Zone

Official religion:	None
Year of founding:	1948
National anthem:	"Aegukga" ("A Song of Love for the Country")
Government:	Multiparty republic
Chief of state:	President
Head of government:	Prime minister
Area:	38,022 square miles (98,477 sq km)
Greatest distance east to west:	185 miles (298 km)
Greatest distance north to south:	300 miles (480 km)
Latitude and longitude of geographic center:	37° N, 127° 30' E
Land and water borders:	The Demilitarized Zone to the north with North Korea beyond; the Sea of Japan to the east; the Yellow Sea the west; the Korea Strait to the southeast
Highest elevation:	6,398 feet (1,950 m) above sea level, Hallasan
Lowest elevation:	Sea level, along the coast
Average high temperatures:	In Seoul, 32°F (0°C) in January and 88°F (31°C) in August
Average annual precipitation:	From 40 inches (102 cm) north of Daegu to 70 inches (178 cm) on Jeju Island

Cheomseongdae

Currency

National population (2007 est.): 49,044,790

Population of largest cities (2005 est.):

Seoul	10,300,000
Busan	3,700,000
Incheon	2,600,000
Daegu	2,500,000
Daejeon	1,500,000

Famous landmarks:
- ▶ *Bulguksa Temple*, Gyeongju
- ▶ *Cheomseongdae Observatory*, Gyeongju
- ▶ *Daecheon Beach*, in the southwest
- ▶ *Gyeongbokgung Palace*, Seoul
- ▶ *Haeinsa Temple*, in the southeast
- ▶ *Hallasan*, Jeju Island
- ▶ *Seoraksan National Park*, in northeastern South Korea

Industry: South Korea's leading industries include shipbuilding and the manufacture of cement, steel, automobiles, computer equipment and parts, textiles, clothing, and shoes. Coal is South Korea's main mining product, and rice is the leading agricultural crop.

Currency: The won. In 2007, US$1 equaled 917 won.

System of weights and measures: Metric and traditional systems

South Korean girls

Ban Ki-moon

Literacy rate:	98 percent

Common Korean words and phrases:

Ye	Yes
Aniyo	No
Annyeonghasimnikka	Hello
Annyeonghigaseyo	Good-bye
Byeoi malsseumyo	You're welcome
Gamsahamnida	Thank you
Eolma imnikka?	How much does it cost?
Sillehamnida	Excuse me

Famous people:

Ban Ki-moon	(1944–)
Secretary-general of the United Nations	
Chung Kyung-wha	(1948–)
Violinist	
Jo Su-mi	(1962–)
Opera singer	
Jeon Do-yeon	(1973–)
Actress	
Kim Dae-jung	(1925–)
President, Nobel Peace Prize winner	
Sun Myung Moon	(1920–)
Founder of the Unification Church	
Park Chung-hee	(1917-1979)
Dictatorial president	
Rain (Jeong Ji-hun)	(1982–)
Pop singer	
Syngman Rhee	(1875–1965)
First president	
Sejong	(1397–1450)
King	
Yi Sun-sin	(1545–1598)
Inventor of world's first ironclad ship	

To Find Out More

Books

- Bowden, Rob. *South Korea*. New York: Facts on File, 2006.

- Dudley, William (ed.). *North and South Korea*. San Diego: Greenhaven Press, 2003.

- *Korea*. Broomall, PA: Mason Crest Publishers, 2003.

- Masse, Johanna. *South Korea*. Milwaukee: Gareth Stevens Publishing, 2002.

Audio Recordings

- *Four Thousand Years of Korean Folk Music*. Pismo Beach, CA: Legacy International, 2000.
  CD with 10 songs showcasing the variety of Korean folk music.

- Hong, Hei-Kyung. *Korean Songs*. Paris: EMI Records/Virgin Classics, 2003.
  CD with 16 songs in the Western classical style sung by opera singer Hei-Kyung Hong.

- *Korean Court Music*. New York: Lyrichord Discs, 1993.
  CD recorded in Seoul with the Orchestra of the National Music Institute.

Video Recordings

- *Asia Rising: Japan and Korea Rebuild*. WGBH Boston, 1999.
  Discusses South Korea's rising economic prosperity from the end of the Korean War to the early 1990s.

- *Families of South Korea*. Master Communications, 2001.
  Compares family life in a village and in Seoul.

▶ *Hidden Korea*. PBS Home
Video, 2001.
Showcases traditional foods, crafts,
arts, and religious practices.

Web Sites

▶ **Korea.net: The Republic of Korea**
Official Website
www.korea.net
For information from the Korean
government about news, the economy,
culture, science, sports, and travel.

▶ **The Korea Times**
www.koreatimes.co.kr
To read Korea's largest English-
language daily newspaper.

▶ **Tour2Korea**
http://english.tour2korea.com
To learn more about South Korean
culture, sights, and news.

Organizations and Embassies

▶ **Embassy of the Republic of Korea**
in Canada
150 Boteler Street
Ottawa K1N 5A6
Canada
613-244-5010
www.emb-korea.on.ca

▶ **Embassy of the Republic of Korea**
in the United States of America
2450 Massachusetts Avenue NW
Washington, D.C. 20008
202-939-5600
www.koreaembassyusa.org

▶ **Korean Cultural Center, L.A.**
5505 Wilshire Boulevard
Los Angeles, CA 90036
323-936-7141
www.kccla.org

Index

Page numbers in *italics* indicate illustrations.

Meet the Author

P ATRICIA K. KUMMER writes and edits educational materials and nonfiction books for children and young adults from her home office in Lisle, Illinois. She earned a bachelor of arts degree in history from the College of St. Catherine in St. Paul, Minnesota, and a master of arts degree in history from Marquette University in Milwaukee, Wisconsin. Before starting her career in publishing, she taught social studies at the junior high/middle school level.

Since then, Kummer has written about American, African, Asian, and European history for textbook publishers. She has also written and edited books about countries, U.S. states, and natural wonders of the world. Her books include *Côte d'Ivoire*, *Ukraine*, *Tibet*, *Singapore*, *Cameroon*, *Syria*, *Jordan*, and *North Korea* in the Children's Press series Enchantment of the World. She also wrote *The Calendar*, *Currency*, and *The Telephone* in the Franklin Watts series Inventions That Shaped the World.

"Writing books about people, states, and countries requires a great deal of research," she says. "To me, researching is the most fun part of a project. My method of research begins by going online. For this book, I found several good Web sites, many of them from departments of South Korea's government. To keep up with events in South Korea, I signed onto a listserv that sent me daily news reports. I also went to several nearby libraries for the most recent books on South Korea."

Kummer hopes that this book will help young people better understand the history of the Korean people and life in South Korea today.

Photo Credits

Photographs © 2008:

age fotostock: 67 (Manfred Gottschalk), 68 (P. Narayan), 21 top, 66, 130 (José Fuste Raga), 84 (Tongro Image Stock), 72, 75 (Travel Pix Collection/Jon Arnold Images)

Alamy Images: 118 (Amanda Ahn/dbimages), 69, 100 (Pat Behnke), 14 (Chad Ehlers), 28 (Matthias Engelien), 119 (Alain Evrard/Robert Harding Picture Library Ltd.), 32 top (Hummel/Blickwinkel), 76 (Jon Arnold Images Ltd), 16 (JTB Photo Communications, Inc.), 105 (Mediacolor's), 121 (Walter Pietsch), 78 (Andre Seale), 120 (Neil Setchfield), 9 (Travel Pix), 8, 12 (Jim West), 40 (Henry Westheim Photography), 7 bottom, 99 (Anna Yu)

AP Images: 7 top, 74, 80, 97, 127 (Young-Joon Ahn), 95 (Jin-Man Lee)

Bridgeman Art Library International Ltd., London/New York: 37 (Gahoe Museum, Jongno-gu, South Korea), 46 (Private Collection/Archives Charmet)

Corbis Images: 53 (Bettmann), 27, 93 bottom, 123 (Massimo Borchi/Atlantide Phototravel), 55 (Patrick Chauvel/ Sygma), 48, 87 (Leonard de Selva), 23 bottom (Robert Garvey), 96 top (Gianni Giansanti/Sygma), 71 (Michael Gore/ Frank Lane Picture Agency), cover, 6 (Tim Graham), 92 (Lindsay Hebberd), 10 (Chan-Sun Hong/epa), 131 bottom (Chan-Sun Hong/epa), 23 top (Jason Hosking/zefa), 117, 133 top (Wolfgang Kaehler), 107 (Christophe Karaba/epa), 65 (Korea Pool/YonHap/epa), 47 (Brooks Kraft), 61 left (Jae-Won Lee/Reuters), 94 (Kevin R. Morris/Bohemian Nomad Picturemakers), 59, 64 (Patrick Robert/ Sygma), 61 center (Franck Robichon/ epa), 91 (Seoul Shinmun/epa), 19 (Michel Setboun), 101 (Paul Souders), 114 (Jim Sugar)

Digital Railroad/Paul Souders/WorldFoto: 115

Getty Images: 93 top (Sandra Behne), 111 (Jae-Ku Choi), 25 (Sung-Jun Chung), 61 right, 133 bottom (Matt Dunham), 54 (Hulton Archive), 112 (Kowoc), 2 (PhotoLink), 63 (Dean Purcell), 15 (Ben Radford), 108 (Torsten Silz), 49 (Topical Press Agency), 109 (Ian Waldie), 62 (Sung-Ho You)

JupiterImages: 13 (Chad Ehlers), 98 (Dallas and John Heaton), 124 (Steve Vidler/ ImageState)

Korea Tourism Organization: 17, 18, 21 bottom, 22, 24, 26, 29 bottom, 32 bottom, 33, 35, 85, 86, 88, 89, 104, 113

MapQuest.com, Inc.: 60, 131 top

Museum of Fine Arts, Boston: 29 top (Maebyeong, Korean, Goryeo Dynasty, Early 13th century, Glazed stoneware with inlaid decoration, Height: 30.8 cm, Charles Bain Hoyt Collection, 50.989), 43 (Perfect enlightenment sutra illustration, Korean, Goryeo Dynasty, 13th century, Colors on silk, 165.0 x 85.0 cm, William Sturgis Bigelow Collection, 11.6142)

NEWSCOM: 45 (Jerzy Dabrowski/Zuma Press), 103 (Ulrich Perrey/AFP), 106 (Vivek Prakash/Reuters), 82, 96 bottom (Yonhap News)

Peter Arnold Inc./Jean-Léo Dugast: 125

Photo Researchers, NY/Terry Whittaker: 30

Rafe Brown: 31

ShutterStock, Inc./Keith Brooks: 70, 132 bottom

The Granger Collection, New York: 90

The Image Works: 77 (Jon Burbank), 110, 116 (Bob Daemmrich), 56 (Fujifotos), 81 (John Nordell), 36, 132 top (Spectrum Colour Library/Heritage-Images), 41 (Topham), 51 (US National Archives/ Roger-Viollet), 34 (H. Winter/SV-Bilderdienst), 58 (Zoriah)

The Trustees of the British Museum: 38, 42, 102

U.S. Department of Defense: 50

Maps and Illustrations by XNR Productions, Inc.

WEST LEBANON LIBRARY
57 MAIN STREET
WEST LEBANON, NH 03784